# Making Dhaka Livable

UPL Monograph Series

# Making Dhaka Livable

Sadiq Ahmed
Junaid Kamal Ahmad
Adeeb Mahmud

 The University Press Limited

**The University Press Limited**
Red Crescent House
61 Motijheel C/A
GPO Box 2611
Dhaka 1000
Bangladesh

Fax: (8802) 9565443
E-mail: upl@bttb.net.bd, upl@bangla.net
Website: www.uplbooks.com

First published 2007

Copyright © 2007. The International Bank for Reconstruction and Development/The World Bank, 1818 H Street, NW, Washington, D.C. 20433.

The material in this publication is copyrighted. Copying and/or transmitting portions or all of this work without permission may be a violation of applicable law. The International Bank for Reconstruction and Development/ The World Bank encourages dissemination of its work and will normally grant permission to reproduce portions of the work promptly.

All queries on rights and licenses, including subsidiary rights, should be addressed to the Office of the Publisher, The World Bank, 1818 H Street, NW, Washington DC 20433, USA; Fax: 202-522-2422, e-mail: pubrights@worldbank.org.

Cover designed by *Ashraful Hassan Arif*

ISBN 984 05 1781 3

Published by The University Press Limited, Dhaka. This book has been set in Century Schoolbook. Designer: Babul Chandra Dhar and produced by Abarton, 99 Malibagh, Dhaka. Printed at the Akota Offset Press, 119 Fakirapool, Dhaka, Bangladesh.

# Contents

List of Tables and Figures — vii
Acknowledgements — ix
Preface — xi

## 1 The Dhaka Challenge — 1
1.1 Overview — 1
1.2 Evaluating Dhaka's Quality as a City — 2
1.3 Objectives of the Monograph — 3

## 2 Evolution of Dhaka's Urbanization — 7
2.1 Primacy of Dhaka — 7
2.2 Dhaka's Population Dynamics — 7
2.3 Poverty Situation — 9
2.4 Economic Activity and Income Base — 11
2.5 Employment — 12
2.6 Delivery of Basic Services — 13
2.7 The Slum Challenge — 20
2.8 Summary on Service Delivery: A Citizen's Score Card — 21

## 3 Constraints to Dhaka's Performance — 23
3.1 Governance of Dhaka City — 23
3.2 An Evaluation of Dhaka City Governance — 28
3.3 Public-Private Roles and Partnerships — 31
3.4 Government Strategy for Reforming Dhaka — 33

## 4 A Strategy for Reforming Dhaka — 35
    4.1 The Imperative for Change — 35
    4.2 The Strategy for Change: Fundamental Reform Principle — 36
    4.3 Rethinking the Governance of Dhaka — 38
    4.4 Managing the Transition: Implementing the Governance Model — 49
    4.5 Key Issues Underlying Strategic Choices — 52

## 5 Concluding Remarks — 55

*References* — 57

*Index* — 61

# List of Tables and Figures

## Tables

| | | |
|---|---|---|
| 1.1 | Top Asian Cities Rated by Asiaweek, 2000 | 4 |
| 2.1 | Gross District Product of Dhaka by Selected Sectors | 12 |
| 2.2 | Year-to-Year Growth of Gross District Product by Selected Sectors | 12 |
| 2.3 | Access to Basic Services in Dhaka Compared with Selected Cities | 14 |
| 2.4 | Percent of All Households Satisfied with Service | 21 |
| 2.5 | Percent of Poor Households Satisfied with Service | 22 |
| 3.1 | Dhaka City Corporation Income | 27 |
| 3.2 | Dhaka City Corporation Expenditures | 28 |

## Figures

| | | |
|---|---|---|
| 1.1 | UN City Development Index (CDI) | 2 |
| 1.2 | The *Economist* Magazine Hardship Ranking | 3 |
| 2.1 | Population Growth of Dhaka Mega City 1980-2015 | 8 |
| 2.2 | World's Fastest Growing Mega Cities | 8 |
| 2.3 | Comparing Growth of Dhaka with Selected SAR Cities | 9 |
| 2.4 | Growth of Asia's Mega Cities, 1980-2015 | 9 |
| 2.5 | Dhaka's Share of Bangladesh's Total Population | 10 |
| 2.6 | Dhaka Division has the Lowest Urban Poverty Rate | 10 |
| 2.7 | … and Highest Growth in Per Capita Expenditure | 11 |
| 2.8 | Inefficiency in DESA/DESCO | 16 |
| 2.9 | Major Problems with DESA | 17 |
| 2.10 | WASA Unable to Meet Demand | 17 |
| 2.11 | Problems with WASA | 18 |
| 2.12 | Breakdown of Sanitation Systems | 18 |
| 2.13 | NMT Main Mode of Travel in Dhaka | 19 |
| 2.14 | Volume of Motorized Vehicle | 20 |
| 3.1 | Multiple Government Agencies are Involved in Providing Services | 25 |
| 3.2 | Responsibilities of City Governments | 30 |
| 3.3 | Centralization of Authority | 30 |

# Acknowledgements

The motivation for writing this Monograph emerged from a concern of the authors, all citizens of Bangladesh, that poor governance is severely constraining the ability of Dhaka to become a quality city. Indeed, the rapid growth of the city unmatched by supply of basic services is fast converting this dynamic city into an unlivable one. Given Dhaka's primacy, this would have serious adverse consequences for future national growth. The Monograph benefited from very helpful comments from Sonia Hammam, William Cobbett, Sandeep Mahajan, Christine Wallich and Shantayanan Devarajan, all colleagues at the World Bank. An earlier version of the Monograph was presented at a seminar in Dhaka in November 2006. We are most grateful to the participants of this seminar for perceptive comments and suggestions that have substantially enriched the quality of the work. In particular, we would like to acknowledge the contributions of Wahidudin Mahmud, Nazrul Islam, Tanwir Nawaz, Salma Shafi, Kamal Siddiqui and Sarwar Jahan. The findings, interpretations, and conclusions of the paper are those of the authors and do not necessarily reflect the views of the Executive Directors of the World Bank or the governments they represent. Errors if any are the sole responsibility of the authors.

# ▪ Preface

With a population of almost 12 million, Dhaka is the capital and largest city in Bangladesh. It is also the 11th largest city in the world. At the same time, it is consistently ranked as one of the world's least livable city. Although income growth is higher and the poverty incidence is lower than the rest of Bangladesh, Dhaka still is a low income city with large numbers of poor when compared with most mega cities of the world. Holding the prospects for better income opportunities than most parts of Bangladesh, rapid migration is causing Dhaka's population to grow much faster than the rest of the country. This fast urbanization is putting pressure on the city's limited land, an already fragile environment, and weak urban services. The population density is now believed to have reached around 34000 people per square kilometer, making Dhaka amongst the most densely populated city in the world.

Poor city management, low efficiency and massive corruption are exacerbating the problems. Urban traffic has reached nightmare proportions, often causing huge delays in covering small distances. Water and air pollution from poor waste and traffic management poses serious health risks. The already acute slum population is growing further, contributing to serious human and law and order problems.

It is obvious that actions to ensure an adequate supply of basic services and to tackle corruption and wastage are needed immediately to avoid a choking of the city's well being. Without improved services, particularly better traffic management, there is a risk that Dhaka's productivity and growth will severely suffer. Importantly, the growing disparity in living standard in Dhaka between the slum dwellers on one side and well-to-do urban elites on the other may lead to increased social and political instability. Evidence from around the world has shown that cities unable to ease such large inequalities in living standards are more likely to face violent events than those that are less polarized.

Given this situation, what are the reform options that will lay the basis for the emergence of a well planned and sound city administration that is responsive to the needs of the residents? The objective of this Monograph is to provide inputs to this city reform challenge based on a solid diagnosis of the problem at hand and drawing on the relevant international experience.

This Monograph suggests that the management problems of Dhaka cannot be addressed in a piece meal fashion. While massive investment will be needed given the large backlog of unmet demand, deployment of additional resources alone will not work. Past experience shows that corruption and mismanagement are serious constraints and unless these are tackled, the effectiveness of additional spending will be limited. As well, given weak fiscal capacity at the national level, much of the new resources will need to come from user fees and greater tax compliance by residents, neither of which will be forthcoming without improved service. So, there is a need to fundamentally and systemically rethink the governance of Dhaka. In this context, the analysis offers some basic guiding principles that must underpin a reform of the city. It provides alternative options and approaches based on a review of good practice international experiences.

The Monograph concludes that in reforming Dhaka policymakers will need to establish a decentralized and accountable city government; that has well defined service delivery responsibilities; has elected government accountable to its residents; has considerable financial autonomy; and has well defined relationship with central government. In sum, Dhaka will need to move towards a well defined city government structure with a strong mayor and council system. Consistent with this broad foundation, actual design will vary based on what might work in the specific social, economic, and political environment of Bangladesh and the Dhaka city. Given the primacy of Dhaka, regardless of the outcome of the forthcoming national elections, the challenge of reforming Dhaka has become a national priority.

Dhaka  
April 2007

**Sadiq Ahmed**  
**Junaid Kamal Ahmad**  
**Adeeb Mahmud**

# 1. The Dhaka Challenge

## 1.1 Overview

With a population of almost 12 million, Dhaka is the capital and largest city in Bangladesh.[1] It is also the 11th largest city in the world. At the same time, it is consistently ranked as one of the world's least livable city. Although income growth is higher and the poverty incidence is lower than the rest of Bangladesh, Dhaka still is a low income city with large numbers of poor when compared with most mega cities of the world. Holding the prospects for better income opportunities than most parts of Bangladesh, rapid migration is causing Dhaka's population to grow much faster than the rest of the country. This fast urbanization is putting pressure on the city's limited land, an already fragile environment, and weak urban services. The population density is now believed to have reached around 34000 people per square kilometer, making Dhaka amongst the most densely populated city in the world.

Poor city management, low efficiency and massive corruption are exacerbating the problems. Urban traffic has reached nightmare proportions, often causing huge delays in covering small distances with associated productivity losses. Water and air pollution from poor waste and traffic management poses serious health risks. The already acute slum population is growing further, contributing to serious human and law and order problems.

All major cities in South Asia are facing similar problems. In general poverty, deplorable condition of slums, corruption and inefficiency in service delivery, weak governance and poor finances are characteristic of all South Asian mega cities: Dhaka, Kolkata,

---

[1] There are some 4 definitions of Dhaka city (Islam, 2005). The concept used here corresponds to the definition used by the Bangladesh Bureau of Statistics to identify Dhaka Mega city. The physical area corresponds to roughly about 1530 square kilometers.

Karachi, Mumbai and Delhi. Dhaka probably ranks the worst, however, in terms of infrastructure, service delivery and city governance (Siddiqui, 2004).

## 1.2 Evaluating Dhaka's Quality as a City

Several agencies have rated the quality of living in major cities of the world. The United Nation's City Development Index (CDI) is considered to be one of the most useful urban indices for comparing cities. The ranking for the latest available year is shown in Figure 1.1. Out of a possible maximum CDI of 100, Dhaka scores 48.4 and ranks near the bottom of the cities ranked. Importantly, Dhaka is ranked below the three other South Asia cities included in the ranking: Lahore, Colombo, and Bangalore.

CDI Components for Selected Cities:

| City | CDI | City Product | Infra-structure | Waste | Health | Education |
|---|---|---|---|---|---|---|
| Stockholm | 97.4 | 93.5 | 99.5 | 100.0 | 94.0 | 99.8 |
| Melbourne | 95.5 | 90.0 | 99.8 | 100.0 | 93.7 | 94.1 |
| Singapore | 94.5 | 91.6 | 99.5 | 100.0 | 92.7 | 88.6 |
| Hong Kong | 92.0 | 89.4 | 99.3 | 99.0 | 90.9 | 81.3 |
| Moscow | 89.9 | 81.0 | 98.7 | 86.8 | 83.8 | 99.3 |
| Seoul | 86.0 | 65.3 | 98.4 | 100.0 | 88.7 | 77.7 |
| Rio de janeiro | 79.4 | 82.3 | 86.2 | 62.6 | 81.9 | 84.3 |
| Sofia | 79.1 | 70.9 | 93.7 | 58.5 | 86.2 | 86.3 |
| Hanoi | 74.2 | 59.6 | 72.0 | 90.0 | 80.6 | 69.0 |
| Havana | 71.0 | 65.0 | 74.8 | 50.0 | 80.7 | 84.7 |
| Jakarta | 69.2 | 66.2 | 57.3 | 46.7 | 80.2 | 95.7 |
| Ulaanbaatar | 68.4 | 53.7 | 59.0 | 90.0 | 72.5 | 66.7 |
| Lahore | 61.1 | 71.1 | 78.5 | 50.0 | 64.9 | 40.8 |
| Colombo | 58.4 | 46.9 | 68.6 | 45.0 | 86.2 | 45.3 |
| Bangalore | 58.0 | 51.1 | 82.7 | 31.3 | 76.5 | 48.5 |
| Dhaka | 48.4 | 55.6 | 45.3 | 27.5 | 64.6 | 48.7 |
| Vientiane | 47.1 | 44.0 | 58.0 | 0.0 | 62.3 | 71.3 |
| Accra | 46.6 | 49.4 | 50.0 | 0.0 | 71.4 | 62.0 |
| Phnom Penh | 43.5 | 40.2 | 33.0 | 27.0 | 47.2 | 69.9 |
| port Moresby | 39.3 | 69.0 | 18.1 | 10.0 | 59.1 | 40.2 |
| Lagos | 29.3 | 42.1 | 29.5 | 2.0 | 44.0 | 29.1 |
| Niamey | 21.7 | 40.0 | 22.0 | 0.0 | 78.3 | 14.9 |

- ☐ CDI Considered to be one of the most useful urban indices
- ☐ Other SAR Cities
- ☐ Dhaka ranks in the lower end, below several other smaller South Asian cities

Source: United Nations Center for Human Settlements, 2001a.

*Figure 1.1: UN City Development Index (CDI)*

The *Economist* magazine also reports a survey of 130 of the world's cities done by the Economist Intelligence Unit (EIU). It looks at 12 factors including housing, education, recreational activities and climate. The purpose is to rank hardships faced by expatriates as indicated by livability. Out of 130 cities ranked, Dhaka received third worst ranking, tied with Lagos (Figure 1.2). Of the four other South Asian cities included in the sample, Colombo, New Delhi and Mumbai all ranked ahead of Dhaka. Only Karachi got a lower ranking (129 as compared with 127 for Dhaka).

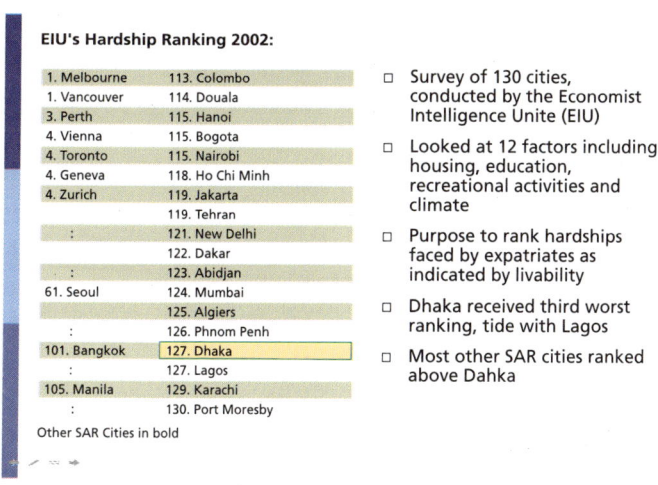

Source: The Economist Intelligence Unit, 2002.

Figure 1.2: The Economist Magazine Hardship Ranking

Dhaka's performance remains weak even when compared with other Asian cities only (Table 1.1). Thus, in the *Asiaweek* 2000 ranking of 40 Asian cities, Dhaka is ranked at number 139, which is only one place ahead of the bottom of the list. Furthermore, Dhaka's rank has been dropping steadily on list: 26th in 1996, 33rd in 1998, and 38th in 1999.

## 1.3 Objectives of the Monograph

It is obvious that actions to ensure an adequate supply of basic services and to tackle corruption and wastage are needed immediately to avoid a choking of the city's well being. Without improved services, particularly better traffic management, there is a risk that Dhaka's productivity and growth will severely suffer. Importantly, the growing disparity in the living standard in Dhaka between the slum dwellers on one side and well-to-do urban elites on the other

## Table 1.1 Top Asian Cities Rated by Asiaweek, 2000

| Country | Ranking | Country | Ranking |
|---|---|---|---|
| Fukuoka | 1 | Kuching | 21 |
| Tokyo | 2 | Cebu City | 22 |
| Singapore | 3 | Guangzhou | 23 |
| Osaka | 4 | Islamabad | 24 |
| Taipei | 5 | Metro Manila | 25 |
| Hong Kong | 6 | Bandung | 26 |
| Bandar Seri Bhagwan | 7 | Bangalore | 27 |
| Kuala Lumpur | 8 | Jakarta | 28 |
| George Town | 9 | Colombo | 29 |
| Pusan | 10 | Chongqing | 30 |
| Seoul | 11 | Delhi | 31 |
| Kaohsiung | 12 | Phnom Penh | 32 |
| Changmai | 13 | Mumbai | 33 |
| Macau | 14 | Kathmandu | 34 |
| Shanghai | 15 | Surabaya | 35 |
| Beijing | 16 | Yangon | 36 |
| Bangkok | 17 | Chittagong | 37 |
| Davao City | 18 | Karachi | 38 |
| Hanoi | 19 | Dhaka | 39 |
| Ho Chi Minh | 20 | Vientiane | 40 |

Source: Asiaweek online, 2000.

may lead to increased social and political instability. Evidence from around the world has shown that cities unable to ease large inequalities in living standards are more likely to face violent events than those that are less polarized (UN-Habitat, 2001a).

Given this situation, what are the reform options that will lay the basis for the emergence of a well-planned and sound city administration that is responsive to the needs of the residents? The objective of this Monograph is to provide inputs to this city reform challenge based on a good diagnostics of the problem at hand and drawing on relevant international experience. The Monograph is organized as follows. The Dhaka Challenge is introduced in Chapter 1. In Chapter 2 the analysis provides a review of the evolution of urbanization in Dhaka with a view to illustrating the magnitude of the city challenge. Chapter 3 analyzes the key constraints that impinge on the city's capacity and effectiveness to deliver services. Against the background of this diagnosis of Dhaka's problems, Chapter 4 offers possible reform options based on the social, political and economic context of Bangladesh and relevant international experience. Chapter 5 concludes with a brief summary.

# 2. Evolution of Dhaka's Urbanization

## 2.1 Primacy of Dhaka

Dhaka is the largest city in Bangladesh, its capital, and also the financial, cultural, and business center of the country. The total urban area of Dhaka spans about 1530 square kilometers (Islam, 2005). About 80% of the garments industry in Bangladesh, accounting for the overwhelming majority of the country's exports, is located in Dhaka city (World Bank, 2005b). Dhaka city contributes to about 13% of the country's GDP. Per capita income and literacy rate are higher in Dhaka than in the rest of the country, and the poverty incidence is also lower.

## 2.2 Dhaka's Population Dynamics

From 1906 to 1991, Dhaka city's area grew by a multiple of 58 and its population grew by a multiple of over 35 (Asian Development Bank, 2000). More recently, Dhaka's population grew from 3.26 million in 1980 to a staggering 10.16 million in 2000. In 2005, its population was estimated to have swollen to 12.56 million (Figure 2.1). Mega cities are defined as those urban centers with 10 million or more people. With a population now exceeding 12 million, Dhaka currently ranks as the world's 11th largest city (Figure 2.2). Dhaka is also the fastest growing mega city in the world along with Lagos, Nigeria.

Within the South Asia region, Dhaka has grown much more rapidly than the other mega cities (Figure 2.3), which has resulted in Dhaka overtaking the population in Karachi. During the decade from 1985 to 1995, the city's population growth rate averaged more than 7% a year, much higher than any other South Asian mega city and substantially higher than Bangladesh's average growth rate. Most of Dhaka's growth was due to migration from rural areas. Although the city's population growth rate is expected to

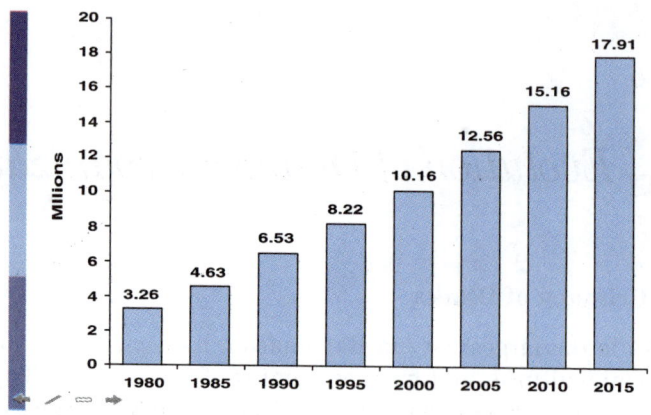

Source: United Nations, 2003.

Figure 2.1: *Population Growth of Dhaka Mega City 1980-2015*

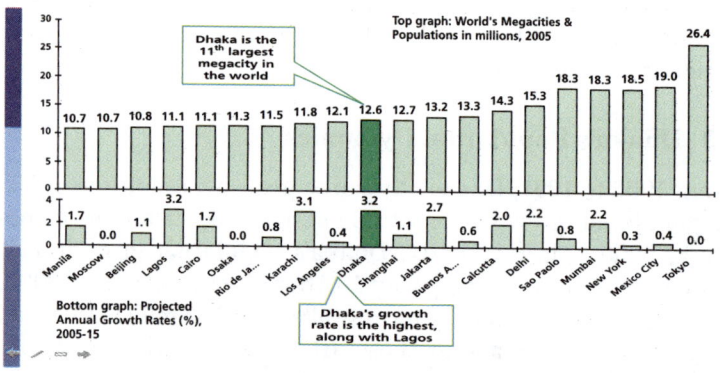

Source: United Nations, 2003.

Figure 2.2: *World's Fastest Growing Mega Cities*

slow down, it is still projected to grow at around 3.2% per annum, as compared with 1.7 % for the country as a whole. If this projection materializes, then Dhaka will become the third largest city in Asia and the sixth largest in the world by 2015 (Figure 2.4).

Due to this high growth rate, Dhaka's share of the country's total population has been steadily growing, currently at over 10% (Figure 2.5). By 2015, almost 13% of Bangladesh's total population, a staggering 22 million people, will call Dhaka their home.

Evolution of Dhaka's Urbanization

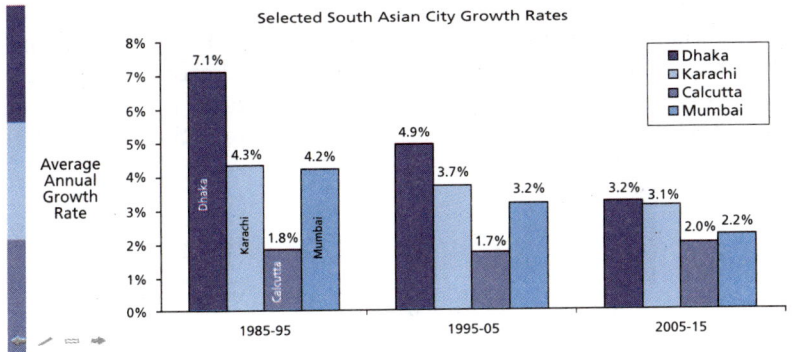

Source: United Nations Center for Human Settlements, 2001b.

*Figure 2.3: Comparing Growth of Dhaka with Selected SAR Cities*

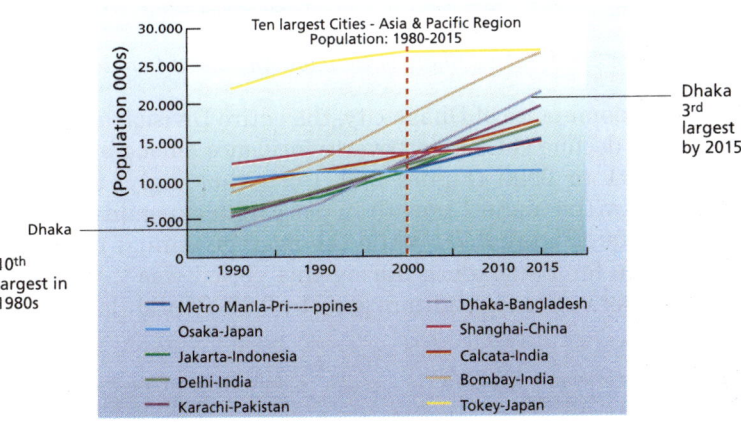

Source: United Nations Center for Human Settlements, 2001b.

*Figure 2.4: Growth of Asia's Mega Cities, 1980-2015*

## 2.3 Poverty Situation

According to the 2000 Household Income and Expenditure Survey, 28% of Dhaka Division's population lives below the poverty line.[1]

---

[1] Dhaka Division is a larger entity than Dhaka city. So the representativeness of the Divisional figures for the Dhaka city is only proximate.

Compared to Bangladesh as a whole, where almost half of the population is estimated to be poor, this is a much brighter picture. When compared with other urban centers, Dhaka Division has the lowest urban poverty incidence, 28.2% compared to the national urban poverty rate of 36.6% (Bangladesh Bureau of Statistics, 2003).

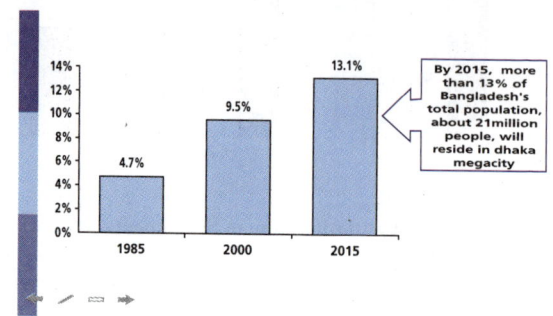

Source: United Nations Center for Human Settlements, 2001b.

*Figure 2.5: Dhaka's Share of Bangladesh's Total Population*

Due to the dominance of Dhaka city, the entire Division experienced the largest decline (14.5%) in poverty incidence among all divisions during 1991 to 2000 (Figure 2.6). Correspondingly, the Dhaka Division saw the highest growth in per capita expenditure during 1991 to 2000 (Figure 2.7). While the average annual increase in expenditure for Bangladesh during this period was 2.4%, Dhaka Division's per capita expenditure grew by 3.2% (World Bank, 2002).

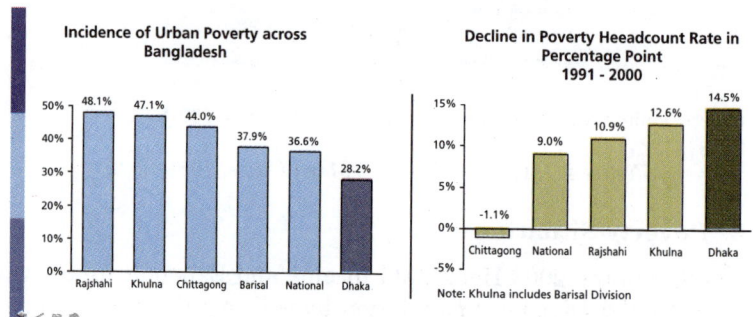

Source: Bangladesh Bureau of Statistics, 2001; World Bank, 2002.

*Figure 2.6: Dhaka Division has the Lowest Urban Poverty Rate*

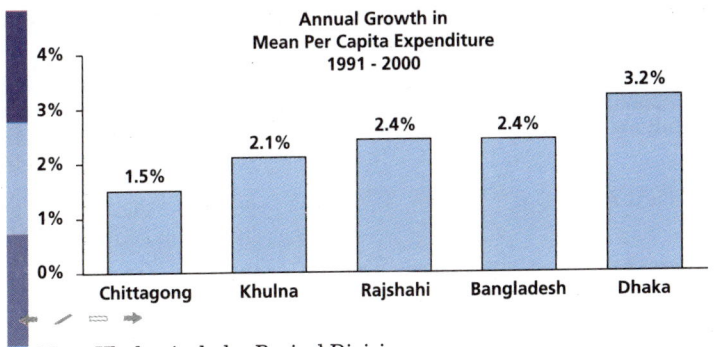

Note: Khulna includes Barisal Division
Source: World Bank, 2002

*Figure 2.7: ... and Highest Growth in Per Capita Expenditure*

Although consumption growth and poverty reduction in Dhaka have been higher than the rest of the country, Dhaka also has much higher inequality. Thus, gini coefficient in Dhaka is 0.37, compared with 0.31 for the country as a whole, 0.29 for Chittagong and 0.35 for Khulna. This inequality is most telling for household consumption, which is 5 times higher for the richest quintile as compared with the poorest (World Bank, 2005).

## 2.4 Economic Activity and Income Base

The economic importance of Dhaka is not surprising given its primacy as the nation's commercial, political, and educational center. In 1999-2000, Dhaka mega city contributed to about 13% of the country's total GDP. This share is now likely to have grown substantially more specially in view of the rapid growth in construction and formal services. Much of the economic activity is in manufacturing and services (Tables 2.1 and 2.2). Most of the country's garments industry has been set up in the city. This industry alone is responsible for almost 80% of Bangladesh's export earnings. Much of the organized service sector (government, banking, construction, and trade) is also concentrated in Dhaka. Because of this concentration of income opportunities, per capita income in the city is much higher than the national average or for other cities in Bangladesh. Thus, in 1999-2000, average per capita income in the city was about $872, which is 2.4 times that of the national average of $363. With similar growth, this would have amounted to $1056 in 2005.

## Table 2.1 Gross District Product of Dhaka by Selected Sectors (in million BDT)

|  | 1995-96 | 1996-97 | 1997-98 | 1998-99 | 1999-00 |
|---|---|---|---|---|---|
| Agriculture | 2540<br>1.0% | 2887<br>1.1% | 3075<br>1.1% | 3036<br>1.0% | 3229<br>1.0% |
| Manufacturing | 84630<br>33.9% | 88404<br>33.6% | 96509<br>34.2% | 100243<br>34.1% | 104822<br>33.9% |
| All Services | 134985<br>54.0% | 142399<br>54.1% | 151857<br>53.7% | 159162<br>54.1% | 168644<br>54.6% |
| Wholesale and retail trade | 39503<br>15.8% | 40682<br>15.5% | 43770<br>15.5% | 44700<br>15.2% | 47170<br>15.3% |
| Transport, storage and communication | 34257<br>13.7% | 37427<br>14.2% | 40361<br>14.3% | 43097<br>14.6% | 46191<br>14.9% |
| Total | 249969 | 263173 | 282557 | 294271 | 309085 |

Source: Bangladesh Bureau of Statistics 2002, 2003; World Bank analysis.
Note: Percentages denote share of total GDP for that sector; components will not add up to total since not all sectors are included.

## Table 2.2 Year-to-Year Growth of Gross District Product by Selected Sectors (in million BDT)

|  | 1996-1997 | 1997-1998 | 1998-1999 | 1999-2000 | Growth from 1996-2000 |
|---|---|---|---|---|---|
| Agriculture | 13.66% | 6.51% | –1.27% | 6.36% | 27.1% |
| Manufacturing | 4.46% | 9.17% | 3.87% | 4.57% | 23.9% |
| All Services | 5.49% | 6.64% | 4.81% | 5.96% | 24.9% |
| Wholesale and retail trade | 2.98% | 7.59% | 2.12% | 5.53% | 19.4% |
| Transport, storage and communication | 9.25% | 7.84% | 6.78% | 7.18% | 34.8% |
| Growth of total GDP | 5.28% | 7.37% | 4.15% | 5.03% | 23.6% |

Source: Bangladesh Bureau of Statistics 2003, 2004.

## 2.5 Employment[2]

Owing to rapid migration and increasing female participation rate, Dhaka's labor force has expanded much faster than the national average. There were an estimated 3.5 million active participants

---

[2] This section draws on the analysis contained in World Bank, 2006.

in the Dhaka labor force in 2000, representing 59% of the working age population in the city (10 years and over), which is 84% of the male and 33% of the female working age population. Services sector accounts for two-thirds of total employment as compared with only 25% for the country as a whole. There is a little bit of agricultural activity on the periphery of the Dhaka metropolitan area but it accounts for some 11 percent of employment. Industry accounts for some 20 percent of employment, of which half are in the garments sector and mostly female workers. This compares with only 10% for the country as a whole.

Not surprisingly, education levels of workers is higher in Dhaka than the rest of the country with more than 50% of the employed population aged 15 plus attaining education of class 6 or above. This compares with only 50% for the country. Also, females constitute a third of the labor force in Dhaka, primarily due to the garments sector, as compared with 18% for Delhi and 14% in Kolkata.

## 2.6 Delivery of Basic Services

The low international ranking suggests that access to basic services is relatively poor in Dhaka as compared with other major cities. This is shown in Table 2.3. Dhaka has done relatively well in providing electricity coverage, but lags substantially behind in other services. The high housing price to income ratio suggests the low affordability of housing, which is a fundamental urbanization challenge. Against the backdrop of this, we look in some depth at the major issues and constraints in the provision of core services in Dhaka

***Housing***: The housing market in Dhaka has been transforming itself quite rapidly in the recent years following the emergence of a fast growing private sector in regards to land development, direct housing supply, and housing finance. While this has eased the housing constraint for the upper middle class, housing problems of the poor and lower middle class, who constitute the bulk of Dhaka's burgeoning population, remain severe.

At the root of Dhaka's housing problem is the exorbitant land price. Although median income in Dhaka is 50 to 100 times lower, Dhaka's land prices are comparable to those in suburban New York or London. For example, land in Dhanmondi residential area is roughly $60 per square feet, which is high even in comparison to the United States where residential land values exceed this price only in the most affluent neighborhoods (World Bank, 2004a). Prices are

**Table 2.3 Access to Basic Services in Dhaka Compared with Selected Cities (1998)**

| City | Ratio of housing prices to income | Access to potable water (%) | Access to sewerage connection (%) | Access to electricity (%) | Access to telephone (%) |
|---|---|---|---|---|---|
| Dhaka | 16.7 | 60 | 22 | 90 | 7 |
| Buenos Aires | 5.1 | 100 | 98 | 100 | 70 |
| Santiago de Chile | n.a. | 100 | 99 | 99 | 73 |
| Abidjan | 14.5 | 26 | 15 | 41 | 5 |
| Yangon | 8.3 | 78 | 81 | 85 | 17 |
| Rio de Janeiro | n.a. | 88 | 80 | 100 | 59 |
| Jakarta | 14.6 | 50 | 65 | 99 | 25 |
| Ibadan | n.a. | 26 | 12 | 41 | n.a. |
| Seoul | 5.7 | 100 | 99 | 100 | 80 |
| Lima | 10.4 | 75 | 71 | 99 | n.a. |
| Bangkok | 8.8 | 99 | 100 | 100 | 60 |
| Casablanca | n.a. | 83 | 93 | 91 | n.a. |
| Damascus | 10.3 | 98 | 71 | 95 | 10 |
| Ankara | 4.5 | 97 | 98 | 100 | 80 |
| Cebu | 13.3 | 41 | 92 | 80 | 25 |
| Lima | 10.4 | 75 | 71 | 99 | n.a. |

Source: World Bank, 2005a.

similarly high in most other residential areas of Dhaka, including the periphery. Because of this, it is impossible to make housing affordable for the poor. Not surprisingly, a heavy concentration of poor has emerged in the slum areas creating all kinds of human and law and order problems (the slum problem is discussed later). The supply of moderately priced housing also is a major issue.

Importantly, the heavy premium on land has made illegal land grabbing and related corruption of land regulatory agencies into a booming business activity. For example, most Dhaka residents who have dealt with the Capital City Development Agency (RAJUK), which is responsible for development of townships and regulation of related land use, believe this to be the most corrupt agency in the country. Accountability for public sector land is poor. Basic enforcement of property rights is also lax.

Another critical constraint to housing is the inadequate availability of housing finance (World Bank, 2004a). In the past, housing finance at subsidized rates was rationed to only the influential clients through specialized public agencies such as the House Building Finance Corporation (HBFC). On a more limited scale, the Nationalized Commercial Banks (NCBs) also provided housing finance again to influential clients. The subsidized rationed access also meant huge corruption in the allocation of these loans. More recently, the private sector has entered this business that has significantly improved the availability and allocation of housing finance. Yet the total availability relative to needs remains low (World Bank, 2005b, 2004a).

A third problem is the mismatch in the supply and demand for different types of housing in Dhaka. As a result of high land prices, better access of the rich to existing types of housing finance, and the influx of illegal money there has been a rapid growth in the availability of upscale housing in the form of luxury to mid-scale apartments in the top residential areas. Much of the demand for these housing reflects efforts to convert illegal money into safe assets. As such supply in the up-scale rental market has increased and rents have fallen in real terms. On the other hand, demand for moderately priced housing continues to outpace supply. Along with efforts to curb corruption and stem speculative housing purchases, resolution of this mismatch calls for more innovative housing finance and regulatory reforms to meet the demand for lower priced housing.

**Electricity:** Electricity is provided by two public electric distribution entities called Dhaka Electricity Supply Authority (DESA) and the Dhaka Electric Supply Company (DESCO). They both buy power from the publicly owned generation entity called Power Development Board (PDB). DESCO has taken over responsibility of affluent areas and northern Dhaka. An estimated 90% of population in Dhaka has power connections, which compares favorably with the rest of the country. Per capita consumption is 45kw/hour and demand is growing at 12% per year. However, there are high system losses, around 20-30%. Load shedding, especially in the summer, is common due to insufficient peak load capacity. DESA's collection efficiency has improved recently, but losses still remain high (Figure 2.8).

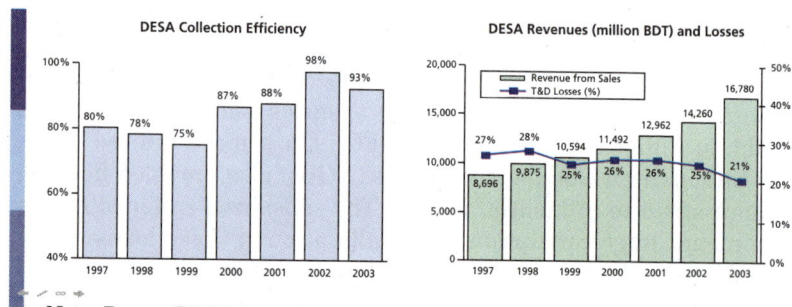

Note: Recent DESCO numbers are similar
Source: World Bank 2004c

*Figure 2.8: Inefficiency in DESA/DESCO*

In addition, bribery and the need to visit DESA offices repeatedly are major problems with service, as disclosed by a World Bank-Proshika survey (Figure 2.9; World Bank, Proshika and Survey and Research System, 2002).

***Water Supply:*** Some 70% of Dhaka's population has now access to piped water, growing from 60% in 1998. Piped water is provided by an autonomous water agency, the Dhaka Water and Sewerage Authority (D-WASA). The D-WASA currently obtains most of its water from an over exploited aquifer. Because of the high rate of population growth, access to piped water seems to be decreasing. Dhaka's groundwater level is rapidly declining due to over-use. It dropped 20 meters in the last decade. Future development of surface

Evolution of Dhaka's Urbanization 17

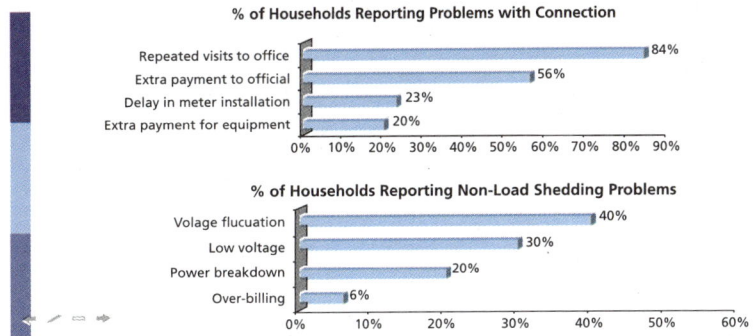

Source: World Bank, Proshika and Survey Research System, 2002

*Figure 2.9: Major Problems with DESA*

water sources is in danger because of industrial pollution. The D-WASA is unable to meet full demand of the city (Figure 2.10). There is high system loss of 40% and collection efficiency is around 80 percent, although deficits have gone down in recent years both in absolute liters and as percentage of demand. There are also significant complaints arising from the long time it takes to get connection, illegal payments, and inadequate supply (Figure 2.11).

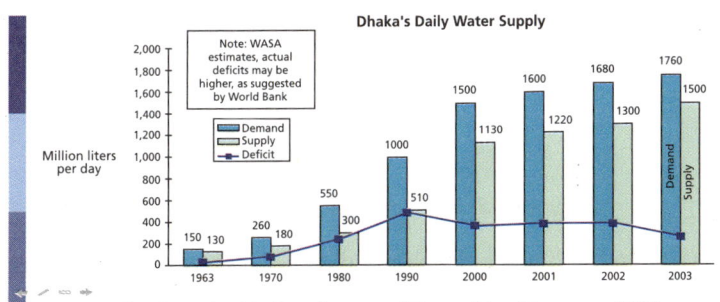

Source: The Sustainable Development Networking Program, 2005.

*Figure 2.10: WASA Unable to Meet Demand*

**Sanitation:** In 1998, only 15 percent of Dhaka's population had access to sewerage connection through D-WASA, while about 30% of the population had no access to any type of sanitation (Figure 2.12). This population basically uses roadside drains or other spaces causing tremendous health hazards through water and air pollution.

18  Making Dhaka Livable

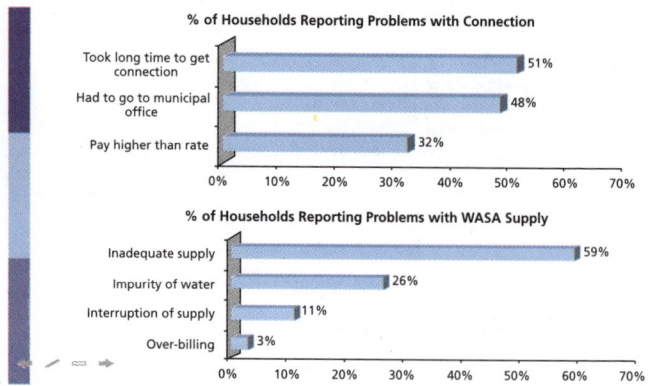

Source: World Bank, Proshika and Survey Research System, 2002.

*Figure 2.11: Problems with WASA*

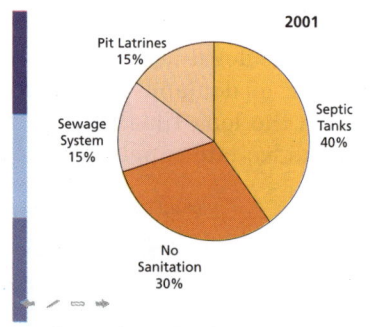

Source: Asian Development Bank, 2001a.

*Figure 2.12: Breakdown of Sanitation Systems*

The system of household waste disposal is similarly inadequate. It is estimated that about 3,200 metric tons of solid waste is produced per day. Only about 50% is collected by the city authority for proper disposal. Overall, the sanitation management is grossly inadequate, posing a tremendous health challenge.

***Transportation:*** The commuting pattern in Dhaka during the late 1990s is indicated in Figure 2.13. In the absence of a public mass transit system, much of the traffic relied on private sources, with rickshaws providing the most used travel mode. It is remarkable that a mega city like Dhaka has relied on walking

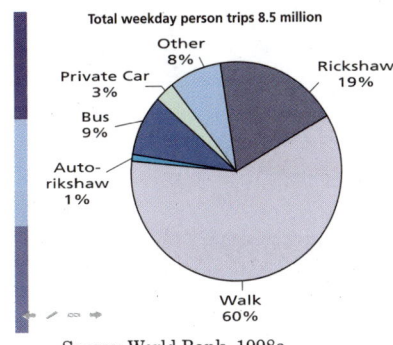

Source: World Bank, 1998a.

*Figure 2.13: NMT Main Mode of Travel in Dhaka*

and Non-Motorized Transport (NMT) as the major method of commute (79 percent). On the positive side, the NMT has lowered the potential air pollution while also conserving energy. Additionally, the rickshaws employ a larger number of poor. On the negative side, NMT has contributed to heavy traffic congestion and poses a severe safety hazard.

The volume of motorized vehicle, however, is rising quite rapidly since the mid-1990s (Figure 2.14). The lack of a mass transit system and unreliable public bus system has spurred the growth of private motorized transport. This growing motorized transport along with continued use of rickshaws is rapidly adding to Dhaka's already serious congestion problem. While attempts have been made to restrict use of rickshaws in a number of heavily used city roads, weak traffic management and inadequate city road network are fast pushing the city into a traffic nightmare. This could seriously constrain the economic growth of the city with associated risks for national growth.

***Pollution***: The main source of air pollution is emissions from vehicles and brickfields. A study by the Bangladesh Atomic Energy Commission found lead pollution in Dhaka to be the highest in the world. The Department of Environment survey cited pollution in Dhaka as "alarming" and found Suspended Particulate Matter (SPM) of over 1700 micrograms per cubic meter (mcg), where the acceptable standard is 400-500 mcg. Noise level is also above the acceptable standard.

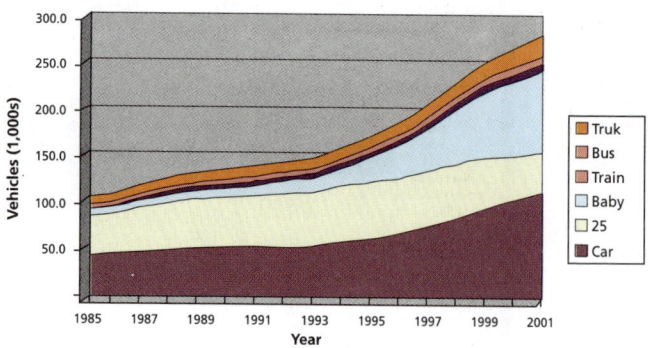

Source: Bangladesh Bureau of Statistics 2001, 2003, 2004

*Figure 2.14: Volume of Motorized Vehicle*

## 2.7 The Slum Challenge

The combination of large numbers of poor (an estimated 3.4 million) and unaffordability of housing have led to a swelling in the number of people living in sub-human conditions in the slums.[3] It is estimated that a third of Dhaka's population live in slums (World Bank, 2005b). The majority of slum dwellers are under the poverty line: earning less than BDT 4,500/month. Some 15% of households earn less than BDT 3,000, 65% earn less than BDT 4,000 per month. Persistent inequalities in women's wages and male control over female labor prevail. Some 53% of husbands do not allow women to work and nearly half of children aged 10-14 are involved in income generating work (Pryer, 2003).

There is an estimated 4966 slum settlements scattered all over the city (Islam, 2005). Living conditions in the slum areas are appalling. Most housing are make shift arrangements with strong vulnerability to frequent sufferings from rain water seepage and flooding. Only 43 of the slums are within 100 meters of public toilet. Most garbage is dumped in the close proximity of the slums, which is rarely serviced. Less than a third of the slum population has access to safe water (piped or tube wells). Only 7% of the slums have a public health clinic and 26% have a government school. In the absence of security of tenure and the persistent risk of eviction,

---

[3] For a recent review of the slum challenge in Bangladesh, see Center for Urban Studies (2006).

the slum dwellers are a frequent prey to the *mastaans* (hooligans) for all kinds of extortions and protection money.

While the slum dwellers are subject to sub-human living conditions and frequent exposure to the whims of the *mastaans*, the slums themselves are also a breeding ground for criminal and violent activities. The combination of drug, alcohol and women trafficking activities in the slum environment pose a substantial law and order problem.

## 2.8  Summary on Service Delivery: A Citizen's Score Card

User feedback provides a useful tool for judging the performance of service providers and thereby helping develop performance improvement strategies and action plans. This "citizen's scorecard" approach is used in many parts of the world (World Bank, Proshika and Survey and Research System, 2002). In the South Asia region, this has been pioneered by the Public Affairs Center (PAC), a non-profit organization, in Bangalore, India. Based on its success, report cards have also been prepared for seven other cities in India — Ahmedabad, Chennai, Kolkata, Delhi, Mumbai and Pune. For Bangladesh, a score card study was done in 2002 jointly by the World Bank, Proshika and the Survey and Research System. The Survey covered 4 major cities of Dhaka, Chittagong, Rajshahi and Khulna. The results are summarized in Tables 2.4-2.5.

### Table 2.4  Percent of All Households Satisfied with Service

| Service Type | Dhaka | Chittagong | Khulna | Rajshahi |
|---|---|---|---|---|
| Police | 2 | 0 | 1 | 2 |
| Land registration | 2 | 1 | 10 | 4 |
| Transport | 7 | 3 | 19 | 6 |
| Electricity | 8 | 2 | 12 | 2 |
| Health care | 11 | 4 | 18 | 9 |
| Garbage disposal | 15 | 10 | 12 | 10 |
| Sewerage/sanitation | 17 | 16 | 11 | 16 |
| Education | 21 | 5 | 28 | 12 |
| Drinking water | 27 | 9 | 11 | 8 |
| Gas | 75 | 29 | – | – |

Source:  World Bank, Proshika and Survey and Research System, 2002.

## Table 2.5  Percent of Poor Households Satisfied with Service

| Service Type | Dhaka | Chittagong | Khulna | Rajshahi |
|---|---|---|---|---|
| Police | 0 | – | 3 | – |
| Land registration | 0 | 0 | 8 | 10 |
| Transport | 2 | – | – | – |
| Electricity | 3 | – | 0 | 8 |
| Health care | 3 | 9 | 21 | 5 |
| Garbage disposal | 5 | – | 15 | – |
| Sewerage/sanitation | 9 | 9 | 12 | 5 |
| Education | 16 | 0 | 16 | 10 |
| Drinking water | 17 | 9 | 16 | 14 |
| Gas | 33 | – | – | – |

Source: World Bank, Proshika and Survey and Research System, 2002.

The results of the Survey are striking and can be summarized as follows:

- For all cities, the scorecard on service satisfaction is generally very low. The only exception is the supply of gas in Dhaka for the non-poor household.
- On average poor households face much worse service delivery than the non-poor.
- In Dhaka, citizens are particularly unhappy with the provision of police, land registration and transport services. The poor households are also very unhappy with drinking water and sanitation services.
- Detailed analysis suggests that illegal payments to either the staff of service providers or the *maastans* are quite common.
- Furthermore, responsiveness of service providers to complaints is poor; as a result citizens prefer to pay a bribe to get the problem resolved rather than lodge a complain and wait forever.

# 3. Constraints to Dhaka's Performance

## 3.1 Governance of Dhaka City

Performance of a city is strongly correlated with the underlying city governance (Lautier, 2006). This is hardly surprising. A city's governance essentially involves sound legal framework assigning rules of business, responsibilities and accountability; a well-defined management structure; clear assignment of responsibility and accountability, and adequate coordination among concerned agencies; financial autonomy; voice and participation by beneficiaries. Let's look at each of these features in the specific context of Dhaka.

*Legal Framework*: The evolution of the management structure of the Dhaka city followed a number of phases. Following the creation of Bangladesh, all existing local bodies were dissolved and administrators were appointed for each of them via Presidential Order No. 7 of 1972 (Siddiqui, 2004). Subsequently, the municipalities were restored via Presidential Order No. 22 of 1973. Formal legal basis for urban local governments was established through the "Pourashaba" Ordinance of 1977. This was amended in 1978 to create the Dhaka Municipal Corporation (DMC). In 1982 the Mirpur and Gulshan municipalities were merged with the DMC. In 1983 a new Ordinance was passed for the DMC, which was renamed as Dhaka City Corporation (DCC) in 1990. Subsequently, the present structure of DCC was established based on the Local Government Law of 1993. This Law established four City Corporations including the DCC. The management structure provided for the following:

- A city Mayor and Ward Commissioners to be directly elected on the basis of adult franchise.
- A number of reserved seats for women commissioners to be elected by city ward commissioners.
- The Mayor becomes the Commissioner of the City Corporation.

- All city corporations are to be divided into zones whose numbers are to be fixed by the Government.

Assignment of functions and responsibilities and rules of business are provided partly by the Ordinance of 1983 and partly by the Pourashaba Ordinance of 1977 (Siddiqui, 2004). The 1983 Ordinance identified 13 functions: public health; water supply and drainage; licensing of trading in food and drinks; care and control of animals; town planning; building control for public safety; maintaining of public streets; public safety; urban forestry; education; promotion of cultural activities; social welfare; and development. Regarding rules of business, while the city corporations have some flexibility in managing their affairs, via the Pourasabha Ordinance of 1977, the Central Government maintains control over all aspects of their functioning (Siddiqui, 2004).

*Management Structure*: Presently, the DCC has three levels: the Ward (the lowest level unit); the Zone (mid level); and the Corporation (the highest body). There are some 90 Wards and 10 Zones. Each Ward is managed by an elected Ward Commissioner. The Zonal heads are civil servants deputed by the government. The Corporation itself is comprised of the elected Mayor, who is the Commissioner of the DCC, the 90 elected Ward Commissioners, 30 women Ward Commissioners, and 5 ex-officio Ward Commissioners from other public entities providing services to the Dhaka city (the Chairman of the RAJUK, the Managing Director of D-WASA, the Chief Engineer of DPHE, Chairman DESA, and the DG Health). The intention here is to ensure proper coordination between the functioning of the DCC and these other public agencies (see more on this point below).

As head of DCC, the Mayor exercises full authority over its functioning. Delegation of authority to lower levels is entirely at the discretion of the Mayor. The Mayor also has the power to over-rule any decision taken by the corporation body. The DCC is required to establish 8 Standing Committees to deal with matters relating to: Finance and Establishment; Education; Health, Family Planning, Sanitation and Drainage; Town Planning and Improvement; Audit and Accounts; Works and Buildings; Water and Electricity; and Social Welfare. Each Committee consists of up to 6 members elected from among themselves by the commissioners. The Mayor is a member of all these committees, although no other commissioner can participate in more than 2. For day-to-day functioning, the Mayor is assisted by a Chief Executive Officer (CEO), who is a senior civil servant appointed by the Government, and department heads appointed by the DCC.

***Assignment of Responsibilities and Coordination with Other Service Agencies:*** Several agencies are in charge of providing basic services in the Dhaka mega city (Figure 3.1). These include: the Dhaka City Corporation (DCC), the Capital City Development Authority (RAJUK); Dhaka Electricity Supply Authority (DESA); Dhaka Metropolitan Police (DMP); Titas Gas; Various Line Ministries (e.g. Land Administration, Public Works, Education and Health); the Bangladesh Telephone and Telegraph Board (BTTB); Bangladesh Road Transport Corporation (BRTC); and the Dhaka Water and Sewerage Authority (D-WASA).

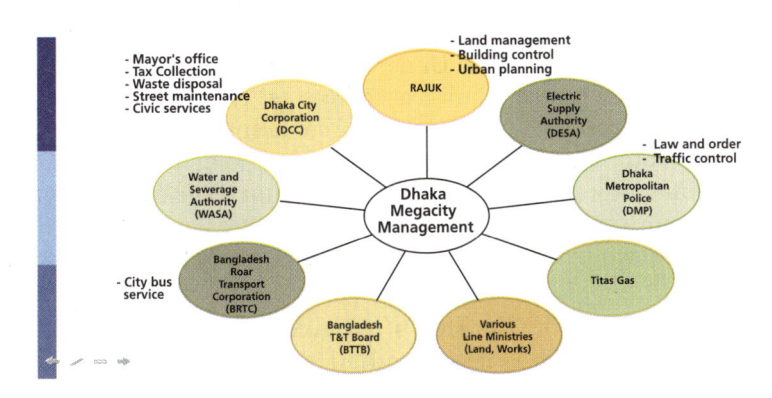

*Figure 3.1: Multiple Government Agencies are Involved in Providing Services*

The RAJUK is an autonomous body under the Ministry of Housing and Public Works. The primary functions of RAJUK are (a) to prepare, implement and monitor a master development plan for Dhaka city; (b) create planned townships including associated infrastructure; and (c) development control and plan approvals for land use within RAJUK areas. The DESA is the major power distribution company serving Dhaka and along with the smaller more recently established Dhaka Electric Supply Company (DESCO) provides all electricity to the city. The Ministry of Power provides oversight to DESA and DESCO. The DMP manages law and order in the city and is managed by the Home Ministry. The D-WASA, an autonomous entity, is responsible for supplying water, drainage and sewerage services in Dhaka. The Department of Public Health Engineering (DPHE) under the Ministry of Health provides oversight to D-WASA. The Bangladesh Road Transport Corporation (BRTC) manages urban transport services in Dhaka and is supervised by the Ministry Communications. Finally, the BTTB provides telecommunications services including in Dhaka, and is supervised by the Ministry of Communications.

It is clear that as a result of multiple service agencies, the opportunities for overlap and conflicts are large. This presents a major coordination challenge. The management structure of DCC noted earlier seeks to address this coordination challenge by incorporating the heads of a few of the above service providers considered most relevant as ex-officio members (from RAJUK, D-WASA, DESA, and DPHE).

***Dhaka City Finances***: Under the Legal Framework, DCC can obtain resources from a number of sources: (a) property tax; (b) rents from markets owned by DCC; (c) fees from licenses issued to traders and non-motor vehicles; (d) fees from advertisements, cinema and entertainment; (e) sale of property/assets and (f) grants and loans from the government. The trend in DCC finances over the 1998-02 period is shown in Table 3.1. The table shows a number of striking features:

- As of FY2002, the DCC's resources were a meager Tk 4.6 billion, which is less than half a percent of GDP and only 2 percent of total government spending. While other service authorities also spend money on Dhaka, this limited resource base illustrates the severe nature of financing constraint for a city government dealing with more than 12 million people.
- Some 59% of total resources are obtained from the government as current and capital transfers and grants, exposing the substantial reliance of the city on the government for funding.
- Of the 41% generated by own resources, property taxes account for about 37%, which is only 15% of total DCC resources.
- The resource pattern has basically remained unchanged over the 4 year for which data are shown in the table.

## Table 3.1 Dhaka City Corporation Income (in million BDT)

| | 1998-99 | 1999-00 | 2000-01 | 2001-02 |
|---|---|---|---|---|
| Market output | 243 | 255 | 260 | 375 |
| | 7% | 6% | 6% | 8% |
| Other taxes on production | 623 | 652 | 658 | 665 |
| | 17% | 15% | 15% | 15% |
| Interest received | 5 | 6 | 6 | 7 |
| | 0% | 0% | 0% | 0% |
| Rent | 20 | 24 | 25 | 25 |
| | 1% | 1% | 1% | 1% |
| Other current taxes | 176 | 200 | 211 | 215 |
| | 5% | 5% | 5% | 5% |
| Current transfers within general government | 469 | 553 | 565 | 572 |
| | 13% | 13% | 13% | 12% |
| Miscellaneous current transfers | 120 | 135 | 140 | 145 |
| | 3% | 3% | 3% | 3% |
| Investment grants receivable | 999 | 1215 | 1260 | 1345 |
| | 27% | 29% | 29% | 29% |
| Other capital transfers | 557 | 630 | 638 | 650 |
| | 15% | 15% | 15% | 14% |
| Disposals of existing fixed assets | 455 | 520 | 525 | 555 |
| | 12% | 12% | 12% | 12% |
| Acquisitions less disposals of land | 20 | 24 | 24 | 25 |
| | 1% | 1% | 1% | 1% |
| **Total** | **3687** | **4214** | **4312** | **4579** |

Source: Bangladesh Bureau of Statistics, 2003.
Note: Percentages denote share of total income for that item.

Looking at the spending pattern (Table 3.2), some 50% are spent on current transactions including salaries and interest payments, while the remaining 50% go for city improvements. While the balance of spending between staffing and city development does not look out of line, there are serious concerns about the quality of this spending as indicated by the citizen's scorecard on service delivery. The outcomes that are achieved from this spending needs careful review.

As noted, the spending by DCC is a subset of total spending on Dhaka mega city. Other service providers such as the electricity authority, D-WASA, RAJUK and DPHE all have separate budgets

## Table 3.2 Dhaka City Corporation Expenditures (in million BDT)

|  | 1998-99 | 1999-00 | 2000-01 | 2001-02 |
|---|---|---|---|---|
| Intermediate consumption | 581 | 775 | 785 | 800 |
|  | 18% | 18% | 18% | 17% |
| Wages and salaries | 548 | 675 | 677 | 790 |
|  | 17% | 16% | 15% | 17% |
| Interest payable | 15 | 22 | 22 | 23 |
|  | 0% | 1% | 0% | 1% |
| Miscellaneous current transfers | 237 | 245 | 250 | 255 |
|  | 7% | 6% | 6% | 6% |
| Investment grants payable | 51 | 260 | 265 | 270 |
|  | 2% | 6% | 6% | 6% |
| Other capital transfers payable | 141 | 150 | 150 | 155 |
|  | 4% | 4% | 3% | 3% |
| Acquisition of new and existing tangible fixed assets | 1147 | 1432 | 1550 | 1555 |
|  | 35% | 34% | 35% | 34% |
| Improvements to non produced assets | 535 | 700 | 710 | 720 |
|  | 16% | 16% | 16% | 16% |
| Costs of ownership transfer on non-produced assets | 12 | 12 | 12 | 13 |
|  | 0% | 0% | 0% | 0% |
| Total | 3267 | 4271 | 4421 | 4581 |

Note: Percentages denote share of total expenditure for that item.
Source: Bangladesh Bureau of Statistics, 2003.

and spend money on city services. A consolidated picture of total spending, sources of funding and effectiveness of spending is not available. This is one area where additional research is necessary. However, the poor quality of services and the large backlog of unmet demand suggest both a serious spending gap and low effectiveness of city spending.

### 3.2 An Evaluation of Dhaka City Governance

***Legal Framework*:** The evolution of the legal framework makes it clear that this has evolved in an *ad-hoc* manner rather than through a systematic approach based on a careful assessment of the effectiveness of the city governments in providing required services. This lack of a vision and a road map to achieve this vision are a major weakness of the legal framework. Consequently, the functions of the city governments including for DCC are not clearly defined, the enabling environment for implementing these functions is weak, and a multiplicity of service agencies often with overlapping mandates has emerged.

**Management Structure**: The DCC suffers from the same centralized management structure as the Government. All authority is vested with the Mayor, who in turn is heavily dependent on the Government for rules of engagement, for the CEO, and most importantly for finances. The remainder of DCC members, especially the Ward Commissioners, has little authority and consequently has limited effectiveness. Inevitably, this has led to heavy politicization of the Mayor position, which basically tends to function as an agent of the government in power.[1] This confused Legal Framework, which allows for elected Mayors and Ward members while providing for heavy government intervention and centralized management, has resulted in poor accountability for services even in a seemingly democratic environment purporting to provide voice and participation to beneficiaries through the voting system.

**Assignment of Responsibilities and Agency Coordination**: This is yet another major problem owing to the multiplicity of service providers with unclear and often overlapping mandates (Siddiqui, 2004). The attempt to provide this coordination by requiring participation of major heads of competing agencies into the DCC decision making process has not yielded much success. More recently, an effort was made to provide this coordination by asking the Minister of local government to chair an inter-agency coordinating committee, but with limited success (Siddiqui, 2004). Experiences from better cities suggest that limiting the multiplicity of agencies is a better arrangement than trying to coordinate a large number of agencies with overlapping functions (Figure 3.2).

**Financial Autonomy**: Arguably the lack of financial autonomy is perhaps the biggest constraint on the effective functioning of DCC. With a resource base of less than half a percent of GDP and relying on the government for some 60% of funding for even this limited resource, it is hardly surprising that a mega city like Dhaka is fast turning into a living nightmare. Decentralization of

---

[1] The exception to this happens when the Mayor belongs to the opposition party, in which case, the effectiveness is reduced by road blocs created by the government in power.

## 30 Making Dhaka Livable

**Comparison of DCC Responsibilities with Selected Asian City Governments:**

| City | CDI | Water | Sewerage | Refuse Collection | Electricity | Telephone | Mass Transport | Road Maintenance | Public Housing | Police |
|---|---|---|---|---|---|---|---|---|---|---|
| DHAKA | 48 | ○ | ○ | ● | ○ | ○ | ○ | ● | ○ | ○ |
| Kathmandu | 62 | ● | ● | ● | ● | ● | ● | ● | ● | ○ |
| Colombo | 58 | ● | ● | ● | ● | ○ | ○ | ● | ○ | ○ |
| Seoul | 86 | ● | ● | ● | ○ | ○ | ◐ | ● | ● | ○ |
| Hong Kong | 92 | ● | ● | ● | NA | NA | ● | ● | ○ | ● |

○ Full responsibility  ◐ Partial responsibility  ● Not responsible

NA: Not available

- Compared to other Asian city governments, DCC ranks in the lower end in terms of centralization of responsibilities
- Many other higher ranking cities have concentration of responsibilities in city government

Source: Asian Development Bank, 2001a, United Nations Human Settlements Programme, 2004.

*Figure 3.2: Responsibilities of City Governments*

fiscal authority to lower levels of government is a challenge any where. But many countries, including in South Asia, have found creative ways of devolving fiscal responsibilities to lower levels of governments including city governments (Figure 3.3). Much of this devolution has happened on the expenditure side, even though bulk of the revenue collection has remained with the central government for a variety of reasons including collection efficiency.

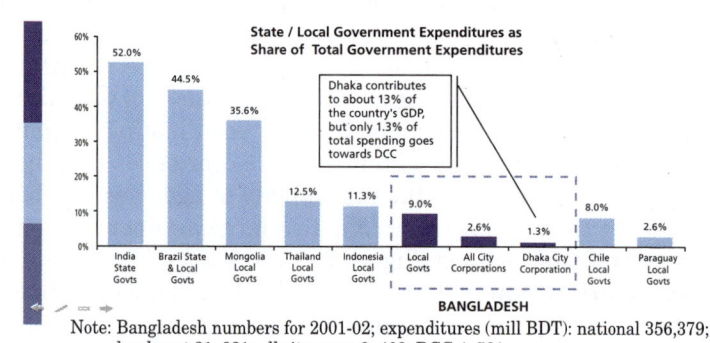

**State / Local Government Expenditures as Share of Total Government Expenditures**

- India State Govts: 52.0%
- Brazil State & Local Govts: 44.5%
- Mongolia Local Govts: 35.6%
- Thailand Local Govts: 12.5%
- Indonesia Local Govts: 11.3%
- Local Govts (Bangladesh): 9.0%
- All City Corporations (Bangladesh): 2.6%
- Dhaka City Corporation (Bangladesh): 1.3%
- Chile Local Govts: 8.0%
- Paraguay Local Govts: 2.6%

Dhaka contributes to about 13% of the country's GDP, but only 1.3% of total spending goes towards DCC

Note: Bangladesh numbers for 2001-02; expenditures (mill BDT): national 356,379; local govt 31, 921; all city corps 9, 402; DCC 4, 581.
Source: Bangladesh Bureau of Statistics, 2002; International Monitory Fund, 2005.

*Figure 3.3: Centralization of Authority*

In the case of South Asia, India is most advanced with fiscal devolution to local governments. For example, in the Indian state of Kerala, the total percentage of Gram Panchayat (GP, rural governments) expenditure compared to state expenditure has more than doubled. In 1993-94 the percentage of GP expenditure to state expenditure was 3.5%, and by 1998-99 it had risen to 7.3%. The government took a proactive approach to devolution, allocating 35% of the budget to local governments. A decentralization planning methodology was also adopted which included data collection at the local government level, setting up sectoral programs with volunteer corps of experts and officials, and preparing a menu of projects from which GPs would choose (World Bank, 2004b). Karnataka is the most decentralized state in India. In fact, the state may have influenced the nation's thinking on rural empowerment, initiated in 1992 through two constitutional amendments.

## 3.3 Public-Private Roles and Partnerships

Capacity constraint to service provision in mega cities is not uncommon. Many cities have found it helpful to redefine its role to provide only those basic services which are in the nature of public good and let private sector handle commercial activities. Thus, services such as electricity, telephone and gas are assigned to private providers with regulatory environment provided by the public sector. In some case, both public and private supply have prevailed allowing consumers choices, thereby improving service quality, while also meeting equity and "merit good" objectives. Examples include: health, education, water supply and sanitation. More and more experiments with this public-private partnership are now underway in South Asian countries. Thus, in Kolkata, toilet blocks have been handed over to the private sector for operation who charges a nominal fee for the use. Partial privatization of street lights and flyovers has also been implemented there (Asian Development Bank, 2000). In Ahmadabad, the slum networking initiative has brought in the private sector to provide all basic physical and social infrastructure services to the 200 slums in the city (World Bank, 2000). The World Bank's slum improvement project in Mumbai has also been very successful by bringing in participation of local slum dwellers to partially pay for their sanitation facilities (World Bank, 2003a).

In Bangladesh, a vibrant private sector has emerged in the delivery of telecommunications, education and health services. In telecommunications, licensing to private providers for wireless telephony is rapidly transforming service including improved access by the poor (Ahmed, 2005). In health and education, private provision, especially in the Dhaka city, is a booming industry. However, these services are relatively high cost and affordability is limited. As well, the regulatory environment for private health services is weak. There is also a strong partnership between the government and NGOs in the delivery of basic education services, which has contributed to important gains in reducing gender disparity and improved overall access to education (Ahmed, 2005). But for other commercial services such as electricity and gas services, they remain public monopolies, and are a major reason for poor service rating in the power sector. The gas sector seems to have fared better although pricing regulations has weakened financial performance and development activities of this important sector.

For core urban services in Dhaka city, such as housing, transport, water supply and sewerage, the picture is also very mixed. The private housing market was long constrained by the lack of housing finance and other regulatory problems. More recently, as a result of progress with banking reforms, the private housing market is emerging as a major activity. This is in terms of both land development as well as finished apartments. The private sector is bypassing the regulatory constraints on registration, permits etc through alleged private payments to concerned public agencies. The problem though is affordability, primarily due to high land prices, but also due to high cost of doing business. Regarding transport, while infrastructure is provided by the public sector, transport service is largely provided by the private sector. Indeed, as noted earlier, the lack of a proper mass transit is a major problem for Dhaka. For private buses, inadequate Dhaka road network, poor traffic management, and weak regulations related to service and safety standards have contributed to low private bus service quality. For piped water the D-WASA has a public monopoly. Private hand tube wells and groundwater extraction through motorized pumps are common sources of water supply for areas not served by D-WASA or where this supply is unreliable. Private water provision as a commercial activity is not present in Dhaka, although illegal private water markets through control over use of public standpipes by *mastaans* are known to exist. Sewerage and garbage disposal is also primarily provided by the public sector (D-WASA and municipality). An organized private service delivery does not exist, although small-scale and informal private services of human waste (pits) and garbage disposal prevail in areas not served by public service providers or as an added community initiative to keep the neighborhood clean.

The lack of private supply of electricity, water and sewerage is a major constraint to the provision and quality of urban services in Dhaka. This tends to exacerbate the problems resulting from poor service from the public providers.

## 3.4 Government Strategy for Reforming Dhaka

The poor performance of city governments including Dhaka has been a source of concern to the government. The frequent attempts to re-define the enabling environment for the Dhaka city government described in Section 2 above are examples of responses to these concerns. Various government documents have also underscored the problems faced by city governments and hinted at solutions to address those problems. For example, in its Fifth Five Year Plan published in 1998, the Bangladesh government recognized the limitations of city and municipal governments and offered a solution. "... more often than not [city governments] depend on other agencies for building up infrastructural facilities and generation of utilities and other services. In a departure from this age-old practice, the present government will encourage and empower the municipalities and city corporations to undertake increasingly more development programs/projects for catering to the needs of citizens." (Government of Bangladesh, 1998, pp. 140) The Government also proposed raising tax bases and delegation of a "substantial share of power of the ministries" to city governments to decentralize authority and increase better accountability and coordination. Unfortunately, little of these initiatives have actually been implemented.

At the heart of the lack of reform is the fundamental problem of governance. Public administration in Bangladesh is heavily centralized. Within the civil administration, almost all authority is exercised by the head of the government and the cabinet. Local governments are very weak, with little administrative and financial authority (Ahmed, 2005). There have been a number of attempts to establish a stronger system of local governments. These have had very limited success due to lack of strong political commitment at the top. Consequently, the setting of expenditure priorities, allocation of resources, procurement of goods and services, and the implementation of projects are largely centralized at the ministry level in the capital city of Dhaka. Even for the limited authority given to the mayors of the 4 large cities, the control of the government in terms of policy setting and finances is overwhelming as noted earlier.

The political progress on decentralization has suffered in Bangladesh from the unsupportive attitude of both the large political parties (Awami League and the BNP), even though the rhetoric has been different. At the heart is the contentious issue of division of power between the national legislators and the local governments. While similar conflicts arise in other countries as well, in Bangladesh this has become particularly complicated because of the small physical size of the country, the homogenous nature of the people and the relative ease of physical mobility. Consequently, national legislators have tended to argue that they can take care of their constituencies without the need for an intermediary political agent (elected and empowered local governments). Civil servants have also found this convenient since this has given them more authority without accountability, especially at the local level.

Very recently, there is renewed debate and interest in exploring options for reforming local governments. Thus, under a new initiative to improve financial autonomy of local governments, the government has introduced a system of block grants in the Annual Development Program. This grant provides a direct transfer of largely untied funds to the Union Parishads of Tk.2,00,000. Although this is a small sum of money, it is based on an explicit recognition of the importance of local decision making and accountability. Other measures taken include revision of local revenue generation procedures and the development of training programs and performance assessment procedures for local governments. On the whole, this is a very small step but in the right direction.

# 4. A Strategy for Reforming Dhaka

Clearly, Bangladesh is yet to come to grips with the reality of the urban nightmare emerging in Dhaka in terms of traffic congestion, urban pollution, rising slum population with associated human and law order problems, unaffordable housing, unreliable electricity supply, and low access and reliability of water supply. The biggest immediate challenge perhaps is the traffic problem which, unless addressed soon, runs the risk of sharply reducing the productivity of the city, thereby jeopardizing the economic growth of the country, given the primacy of Dhaka for economic activity, employment and decision-making. This task of making Dhaka more livable is a core challenge. What are the possible options? In this Section we look into this subject based on relevant international experience.

## 4.1 The Imperative for Change

Dhaka's primacy is largely a reflection of urbanization resulting from expanding economic opportunities, although poor and unbalanced urban planning may have played a role in the growth of Dhaka relative to other urban centers (World Bank, 2006). Growing urbanization in Bangladesh, like in other expanding economies, is a reflection of economic growth and transformation happening from growing opportunities linked to a move from a traditional agro-based economy to a more modernized manufacturing and services based economy. The underlying expansion of employment and income opportunities are a major source of poverty reduction. However, the lack of a well-thought out urban strategy for Bangladesh in general and a city development strategy for Dhaka in particular could seriously erode the productivity and return to investment, thereby constraining growth and job creation.

One important debate concerns the possibility that making Dhaka more efficient may be self-defeating if the improved governance of the city leads in turn to "excessive migration" — a vicious cycle of sorts. There are a number of reasons why this concern is not based on a strong foundation. First, as noted, rural-urban migration is a fact of development. Indeed, urbanization is a metric of economic development. It is not an issue of stopping the migration process but managing it better. In other words, an efficient Dhaka would be better able to manage the process of in-migration and this may well result in allowing the city to accommodate more migrants. Second, by improving the functioning of land, housing and transport markets and proper pricing of services the cost at the margin imposed by new migration could be more effectively passed onto the migrant, thus ensuring a self regulating migration process. Third, the issue of excessive migration needs to be addressed by understanding the dynamics of the overall urban hierarchy in the country. The support for secondary towns — where the growth is actually increasing — will help balance the allocation of population across the country. This is best undertaken by increasing the productivity of agriculture which creates the demand for secondary towns through economic linkages. It also occurs by improving the local governance of smaller towns using the same reform principles used to propose the governance changes for Dhaka (see below).

## 4.2 The Strategy for Change: Fundamental Reform Principle

The resolution of Dhaka's multi-faceted challenges is a daunting task but quite resolvable provided the task is approached in a holistic manner. Piece-meal and incoherent reforms will not do. The magnitude of the service gap as well as continued strong growth in the city's population and income calls for sound planning, strong coordination, huge investment and a solid implementation plan. The present poor management along with hesitant and weak city reforms of the past shows clearly that the status quo or piece-meal changes will not make a difference. A clear long-term vision about the transformation of the city, say in the next 10 years or less, backed by a well thought out strategy, a time bound action plan and a credible implementation mechanism are all essential. This will require strong political will and leadership.

***Improving City Governance is at the Heart of the Reform Strategy:*** The reform strategy in the first place must seek to address the key constraints to the effective functioning of the city government: unclear mandate and service responsibilities; lack of accountability; weak finances and financial autonomy; proliferation of service agencies with poor coordination and control; and weak management. These problems cannot be resolved by tinkering at the margin; they clearly call for a major rethinking and wholesale change in city management and its enabling environment. *Fundamentally, the Monograph argues that key functions will need to be devolved to city governments and, in turn, city governments should be organized to best manage these functions — a two step process that will need to be sequenced and managed jointly between central and city governments in a strategic way. Embedded in this approach is the assumption that strengthening voice — the ability of citizens to reveal their preferences and hold their government to account — will be essential in sustaining the reform of Dhaka city.* It is important to note, however, that devolution is a means to an end and not an end in itself. So, establishing a devolved city government by itself will not ensure the successful delivery of services that the residents of Dhaka will want. However, without an elected and accountable government with clearly defined service responsibilities and clearly identified sources of finance, it is not likely that Dhaka can be turned around to be a dynamic city and provide the basis for continued rapid growth.

One issue where there is some debate is regarding governance improvement versus greater investment for city services. The low access and poor service quality and the backlog of demand for services suggest large funding needs. Transport, power, water and sanitation all require capital intensive enterprises and require large investment. The argument here is that governance improvements take time and the city cannot wait. We believe this is a false trade-off. The past experience provides clear evidence that given the serious corruption, inefficiency and coordination problems it is not obvious that more money alone without improvement in city management will result in sustained service improvement. Additionally, the country's fiscal situation is severely constrained. Much of the additional funding will need to come from service charges. As well, resident's willingness to pay city taxes will depend upon services provided. So, financing and governance improvements are intimately related. Indeed, a part of city reform strategy is to develop viable city government that is able to attract private investment and mobilize public resources based on service delivery and attractive city environment.

Ultimately, the choice of a reform process for restructuring Dhaka and the final models of governance will be determined by political factors and political accommodation. Yet, it must also be recognized that any serious reform option for Dhaka must allow for a fundamental change in the city governance. Against the backdrop of the above, we offer below a framework for assessing the various choices that may finally emerge from a political process.

## 4.3 Rethinking the Governance of Dhaka

Designing the architecture for governing Dhaka is an exercise in political economy whose urgency is well accepted by citizens across the political spectrum, but less so by policymakers. In particular, which model of governance would work and what process should be adopted to engage the various stakeholders in a collective dialogue are questions on which consensus is lacking. The political dialogue on reforming the governance system of Dhaka will need to be informed by three important policy dimensions:

- decentralization of authority and responsibility to cities;
- the design of metropolitan governments; and
- the management of a transition towards a new system.

***Decentralization of Functions and Responsibilities:*** The principle of decentralization of functions seeks to clarify which public functions are best managed at which tier of government. Public finance literature provides a clear strategy for allocating functions to a lower tier of government. Based on notions of economies of scale and spatial incidence of benefits certain public expenditures, such as water distribution, sanitation services, solid waste management, local roads management, traffic management, certain aspects of transport services, are best placed at the local level. These have traditionally been part of the responsibility of urban local governments in many parts of the world.

Underpinning the public finance approach is the principle of accountability, which essentially asks the question who is accountable for the management of public services. In the context of Dhaka we saw earlier that there is no clear line of accountability and responsibility for managing services in Dhaka is dispersed. Indeed, the enabling environment does not put the full accountability for Dhaka's management in the hands of the mayor and the city council. For example, water and electricity distribution — two important services that influence the welfare of the citizens of Dhaka — are in the hands of the central government. Land management — traditionally a core function of an urban government and which influences the spatial setting of Dhaka and the efficiency with which urban services are managed — belongs to a large measure to RAJUK, another central government authority. The policing function — intrinsic to security and protection of property rights — also responds to the edicts of central government.

But the dispersion of accountability is not necessarily inconsistent with public finance principles. If different services are best managed at different tiers of government, then by definition citizens will need to hold a variety of policy makers across tiers of government accountable for public services. In addition, the picture of Dhaka with its dispersed accountability is not atypical of many cities in developing countries. In Delhi, land management is significantly influenced by the central government's Ministry of Urban Development. In Manila, the Water Board — currently under private management — is under central authority. In Johannesburg, a city where issues of safety and security looms large in the concerns of residents, a major part of the policing services is under the direct control of central government. In all these cities, service improvements have happened — and in some cases in a dramatic fashion — even within a context where authority and accountability is dispersed by different tiers of governments. So should we be overly concerned that the mayor of Dhaka is not fully responsible for all the services that determine the well-being of residents of Dhaka?

In many ways the answer to the question whether functions should be devolved to a city government depends on our interpretation of how institutional reforms can be catalyzed. In the context of Bangladesh, where central government itself is faced with many challenges of management and governance, the improvement of Dhaka will depend on the propensity of central authorities to engage in reforms. The Manila Water Board reform is an example of how reformers at the central government level transformed the water board. But Bangladesh is one of the most centralized countries in the world where policy making, service provision and regulatory functions are often under the purview of central government. With judge and jury in one place, the incentive to undertake reform is less and, not surprisingly, the incentive to ensure accountability is limited — self regulation is rarely a forte of public sector. Separating functional responsibility between different tiers of governments therefore creates better incentives for checks and balances between different tiers of government and offers the possibility that the tier of government not responsible for local service delivery — by definition central government — will be in a position to provide incentives for the reform of the system. When central government is the policy-maker, provider and regulator — all in one — it has less incentive to engage in reforms and hold itself accountable. Decentralizing functions to the city level therefore needs to be an important consideration in the reform of Dhaka.

The push for decentralizing authority to the city level is further strengthened by the need to coordinate the management of services in a city — especially given the size of Dhaka — and to avoid undertaking capital investments in a piece meal fashion, one project at a time. For example, the management of traffic congestion — a critical urban challenge for Dhaka — is not a function of a series of fly-over projects only. It is a joint function of urban land management, in particular zoning and land planning, broader regulation of the transport market, management of traffic police, and finally physical investments in road infrastructure. If different aspects of this policy chain are under the purview of different tiers of government, the ability of Dhaka to coordinate its traffic movement will depend on the bureaucratic ability to coordinate public sector agencies. It would be far easier for Dhaka to manage traffic congestion if it was accountable for the policy chain that influences traffic systems.

The example of traffic management can be generalized even more. Cities around the world today account for a mass of humanity living in a close space where they are inter-linked in many economic and social ways. The ability of city managers to coordinate fiscal, regulatory and administrative systems which influence the efficiency of cities is crucial to improving the welfare of urban citizens. In this context, cities need to be managed as stand alone economies where project investments are planned in the context of a coherent city strategy and better understanding of how urban markets perform overall. Where city managers do not have the authority for managing the city as a whole — as a self-contained system — the ability to leverage the productivity of the city to improve the welfare of residents will be limited. Seen from this perspective also, the decentralization of responsibilities and functions to the city level becomes a prerequisite for managing cities more effectively.

The principle of devolution also relates to the tax side of city management. A separate tier of government needs to have the autonomy to raise its own finances and fund its expenditure responsibilities. In the case of city governments the access to property taxes and some form of "neutral" business or income tax is important for ensuring their accountability. Economic efficiency may require that upper tier governments set the tax base, but the principles of accountability and allocative efficiency suggest that the ability to set rates should be devolved to each sub-national tier.

Finally, the support for the principle of decentralization lies in the concept of voice. Urban reforms are often undertaken to enhance the relationship of accountability between the policy maker and the provider — compacts — or between the consumer and the provider — client power. In certain cases, the focus has been on voice — the ability of citizens to hold the state accountable for decision-making.[1]

For example, the reform of the Cochabamba water board, owned by central government, focused on decentralizing operational authority to the water provider. The focus was on bringing clarity of roles between policy makers — in this case central government — and the provider (compact). Part of this step was to contract a private provider to manage the water board. In proposing greater operational autonomy, the reform process was also enabling the provider to have greater flexibility to respond to the needs of the consumers. In particular, the provider would have the ability to raise user charges, thus establishing a direct relationship with the consumer and for the consumer to influence the provider (client power). But, the process of reform placed less emphasis on engaging the residents of the city in the policy decision-making process. The mechanisms of voice — the ability of citizens to hold the state accountable for policy — was not as well established and was partly responsible for the ultimate failure of the Cochabamba water reform.

---

[1] This framework is adopted from World Bank (2003b).

The basic premise of decentralization to the local government level is to bring government closer to the citizen and allow citizens to have a better ability to hold their local government to account. Seen from this perspective, the emphasis on voice requires a shift to a different system of governance — one which allows the preferences of citizens to determine the path of service delivery reform. In other words, decentralization enables voice to determine compacts and client-power.

***Design of Metropolitan Governments***[2]: Devolving authority to the city level raises the important question of how to organize a city government to manage responsibilities placed at the city level. In other words, decentralization of responsibilities is a necessary but not sufficient condition for achieving improved service delivery. What is required in addition is the organization of the local government that is capable of providing the necessary services in a decentralized framework?

The options facing Dhaka could range from some form of non-metropolitan government to different forms of metropolitan governments with either economic or political decentralization as the guiding principles for organizing the city. Below we outline the various options and suggest a set of criteria to judge the appropriateness of these options for Dhaka.

- *Non-metropolitan Model*: A city of 12 million plus spread over an area as wide as Dhaka can be arranged as a series of contiguous municipalities each with its own set of devolved responsibilities, services, tax bases and management system. In this model Gulshan, Dhanmondi, Dhaka central, and Uttara for example can be self-contained municipalities, each with its own mayor and council. Washington DC and its surrounding suburbs that are municipalities in their own rights is an example of how a contiguous set of municipalities can loosely form a broader metropolitan area.

- *Metropolitan Model*: An alternative model is to formally and legally merge all municipalities into one jurisdiction — a metropolitan government where the residents of the urban area would directly elect a mayor and a council of city members. All urban functions would be managed by this one city government. The cities of Toronto in Canada and

---

[2] For more details see Ahmad (1998).

Johannesburg in South Africa have adopted a version of model. Both Toronto and Johannesburg have redrawn their city boundaries to incorporate surrounding municipalities into one city government.

***Metropolitan Model: Economic Decentralization.*** The City of Johannesburg, however, further evolved its metropolitan government along the principles of economic decentralization, offering an alternative system of metropolitan governance for cities. Essentially, in this model, the city government is structured as a metropolitan government, but it does not organize its systems of service delivery in the form of traditional line departments. Instead, the city establishes service delivery under formal corporations owned by the city. Water distribution in Johannesburg, for example, was transformed into a water corporation along the principles of Companies Act, owned by the city, but managed by an independent board and CEO on behalf of the city. In addition, Johannesburg contracted-in a private company to manage the water corporation for a specified number of years. Solid waste was also formed into a corporation, owned by the city but without contracting the management to a private firm.

While water and solid waste represent services with user charges — more akin to private goods — which enabled a corporation structure to be formed, Johannesburg also innovated in services that are dependent on local taxes. For example, road construction, traditionally more suited to a line department organization was also structured to mimic a corporate system. Formal contracts were given to teams within the department with delegated budgets and their outcomes were measured against indicators based on performance of private contractors. Even aspects of treasury, such as debt management, were outsourced and performance benchmarked against returns on the stock market. *In sum, the city became a policy maker and a regulator with service management delegated to corporations or line departments set up as corporate entities or structures that were proxies of corporations.*

***Metropolitan Model: Political Decentralization.*** Some metropolitan governments are structured in two-tiers: a metropolitan tier overseeing a series of separate municipalities. The metro tier and the municipalities jointly form the metropolitan government. Functions can be separated between the two tiers depending on principles of public finance with services that require economies of scale — e.g. network systems — placed at the metropolitan level.

## Model 1: Economic Decentralization

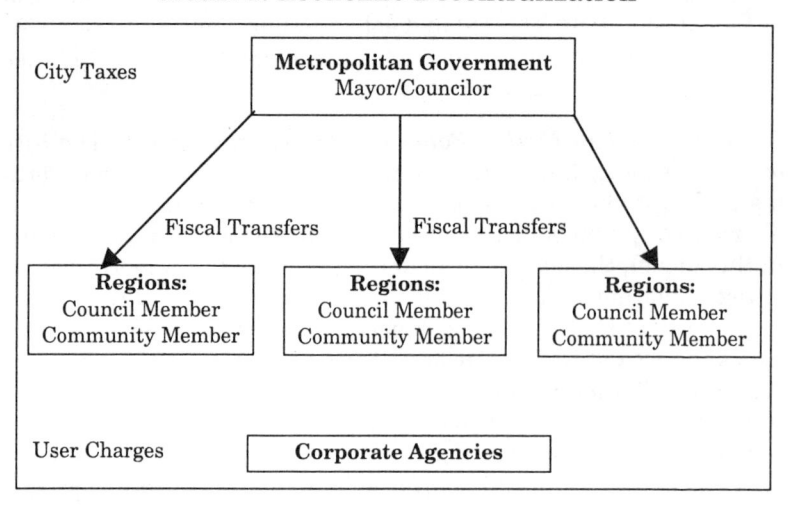

```
City Taxes     Metropolitan Government
               Mayor/Councilor
                   │
         ┌─────────┼─────────┐
    Fiscal Transfers   Fiscal Transfers
         ▼         ▼         ▼
    Regions:   Regions:   Regions:
    Council    Council    Council
    Member     Member     Member
    Community  Community  Community
    Member     Member     Member

User Charges    Corporate Agencies
```

Services that do not exhibit scale economies, such as solid waste collection could then be placed efficiently at the level of municipalities. Land fills, which have scale economies, on the other hand, could be placed at the metro level. Similarly, tax instruments can be allocated between the two tiers on the basis of spatial incidence. For example, personal property taxes could be delegated to municipalities while commercial property taxes whose incidence is beyond narrow municipal boundaries are better placed at a broader, metropolitan level. Pakistan's city districts are modeled as two-tier metropolitan tiers. Minneapolis-St. Paul, the twin cities in Minneapolis, is also structured as a two-tier system with the metro tier playing the function of a pure redistributive tier.

Ultimately, a two-tier political system provides an internal check and balance within a large city government system. It is based on the notion of political competition between different tiers to avoid the emergence of what Buchanan (1975) would label as a "leviathan" city government. A two-tier system is also consistent with a model of metropolitan government with economic decentralization. If Johannesburg were a two-tier model, for example, the city could easily corporatize its water system and make the metro and municipal co-owners of the company. Similarly, in a two-tier system, solid waste collection, best placed at the municipal level, could also be contracted out.

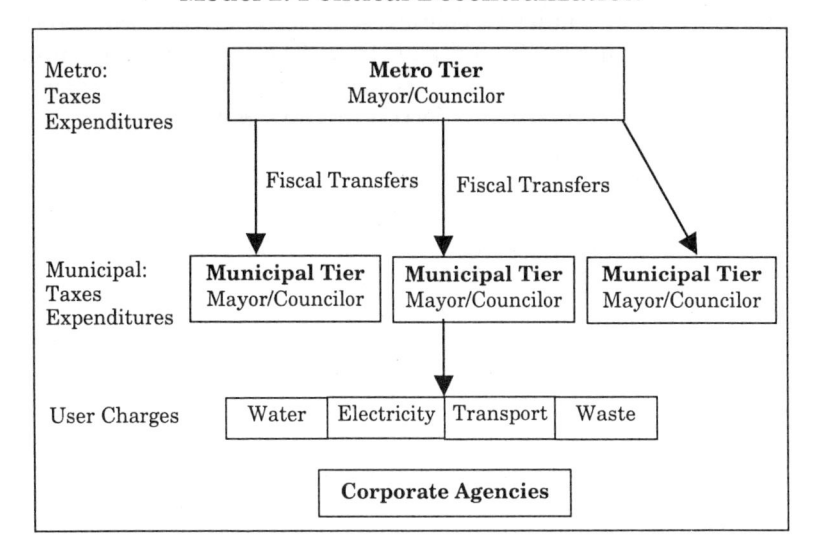

## Model 2: Political Decentralization

```
Metro:              Metro Tier
Taxes               Mayor/Councilor
Expenditures

                    Fiscal Transfers    Fiscal Transfers

Municipal:      Municipal Tier      Municipal Tier      Municipal Tier
Taxes           Mayor/Councilor     Mayor/Councilor     Mayor/Councilor
Expenditures

User Charges    Water | Electricity | Transport | Waste

                        Corporate Agencies
```

***Criteria for Assessing the Models of Governance***: Several important criteria can be used to rank the different models of urban governance. For simplicity, the criteria are summarized along Musgrave's (1959) principles for assessing the efficiency of public finance allocation, namely efficiency, equity, and macro-stability.

*Efficiency*: This criterion is best assessed along three dimensions, allocative, locational, and planning efficiency. *Allocative* efficiency in the urban context can be broadly defined as the ability of the governance structure to reflect the preferences of residents in the allocation of public resources, a factor traditionally described as voice in the accountability literature. *Locational* efficiency is an indicator of whether locational decisions of households and firms are based on economic efficiency grounds or influenced by tax and regulatory decisions of governments with the ensuing deadweight costs. In the context of cities, locational decisions of households and firms can potentially have an important impact on the economic and fiscal potential of cities. Finally the *planning* criterion is a measure of administrative efficiency and, in particular, the ability of cities to coordinate and manage urban affairs.

A metropolitan structure of governance with wider boundaries and devolved functions is ideally suited to internalize externalities. Coordination and planning is easier and locational decisions of households and firms *within* the metropolitan boundary will not be affected by tax or regulatory policies as the latter are uniform across the jurisdiction in a metropolitan setting. The size of metropolitan governments and their structures may however make it difficult for ensuring voice and for reflecting the diversity of preferences that characterize large cities.

In contrast, a non-metropolitan system with separate but neighboring municipalities linked through markets — e.g. labor and transport markets — are smaller in size and better able to reflect voice and represent different household preferences. In fact, from Gulshan to the Motijheel, there is already a self-selection of household residential patterns which reflect different socio-economic strata. Creating and empowering municipal governments around these strata would enable mechanisms of voice to be more effective. But, non-metropolitan systems have the disadvantage of not being able to capture the potential scale economies in service delivery or to ensure effective planning and coordination across a metropolitan boundary.[3] There may also be an incentive to enter into inefficient tax competition as surrounding municipalities attempt to use tax benefits to attract firms into their neighborhood and in the process distorting locational choices of firms and households. Minneapolis-St.Paul is an example of a municipal context where adjacent municipalities engaged in inefficient competition to attract businesses into their jurisdictions. In response, the municipalities created a metropolitan tier of government to pool their commercial taxes and share the revenues on the basis of fiscal capacity. The sharing of commercial taxes eliminated the competition as access to revenues by different municipalities was guaranteed by the metro tier regardless of the locational decisions of firms.

A two-tier metropolitan system — the political decentralization model — offers an alternative way for reflecting voice in a metropolitan organization. By allowing for municipal structures under a metropolitan tier, a two-tier system ensures that a tier of government is as close as possible to the residents. In addition, a two-tier

---

[3] French municipalities — especially small towns — have resolved this problem by entering into inter-municipal compacts. For example, a cluster of towns own a common utility. This is an example of a bottom up coordination and collaboration between municipalities to address issues of coordination. A non-metropolitan solution may therefore be feasible in a context where such inter-municipal arrangements can be promoted efficiently.

system and multiple municipalities within a metropolitan boundary allow residents to access competing political structures. In principle, this should allow for voice to better inform public decision-making. City of Johannesburg adopted a single tier metropolitan structure but addressed the voice issue by following the model from Melbourne. In this approach the city is divided into regions — not municipalities. Council members are then formally appointed to manage the relationship with residents through these regional structures. The size of the regions, whether there are formal consultation structures underpinning the regions, whether the consultations are linked to the city's budget cycles and whether council members have access to budgetary resources are factors that will determine the effectiveness of voice mechanisms.

In sum, the locational and administrative efficiencies suggest a metropolitan model may be superior to the alternatives. Allocative efficiency, on the other hand, favors smaller size urban governments. However, the design of metropolitan governments can be adapted to ensure that voice and, therefore, allocative efficiency is not compromised.

*Equity*: Municipalities are rarely equal in their fiscal capacity. The clustering of poor households and locational choices of firms may result in different municipalities having very different fiscal endowments. The most challenging configuration is when low fiscal capacity and clustering of poor becomes the outcome of inefficient competition between neighboring municipalities. In this context, as in the case of Minneapolis-St. Paul, a metropolitan structure can act as an equalizer by pooling fiscal resources and providing fiscal transfers to different municipalities thus ensuring some level of inter-jurisdictional and inter-personal equity within a metropolitan system.[4] A non-metropolitan system with contiguous municipalities will therefore need an upper tier government to manage the equalization — however defined. Attempts by an individual municipality to engage in redistributive functions would lead to influencing the locational decisions of households and firms with the possibility that at the margin the municipality would attract low-income households seeking the benefits of redistribution

---

[4] This function is similar to the role a central government often plays in an intergovernmental system by equalizing fiscal capacity between different tiers of government.

and the flight of firms or high income households seeking to escape the tax burden.

Equity factors played an important role in Johannesburg's decision to establish a metropolitan structure. Similarly, the problem of the inner city poor and flight to the suburb have led many US states to approve legislation that allows large cities to have "elastic" boundaries. In other words, the States have enhanced the ability of cities to incorporate surrounding municipalities.

*Macro-stability*: In assessing macro implications of multi-tiered governments, Musgrave's emphasis on stabilization was simply to point out that that central government has the comparative advantage in using fiscal instruments to manage macro-economic stabilization. This is well accepted principle in policy making. However, for the purpose of this paper, macro-stability has an alternative focus. In certain context, excessive borrowing by sub-national governments or more generally inefficient fiscal management by lower tiers of governments may result in upper-tier governments providing bailouts. This situation is defined by what is known in the literature as "soft budget constraint." Managing soft-budget constraints is an important policy parameter of central governments in a multi-tiered system of governance.

In the context of this Monograph, the question to ask is whether any particular structure of urban governance has a greater propensity to create a problem of moral hazard and bailouts. The saying "too big to fail" may well be applicable here. One can hardly expect the Government of Bangladesh to ignore a situation whereby a metropolitan government of Dhaka or Chittagong is going bankrupt. The macro-economic costs may be too high. Large, metropolitan governments may therefore be more prone to the problem of moral hazard. On the other hand, a central government may be able to resist policy intervention if the fiscal problem concerns a smaller municipality.[5] This line of reasoning suggests that a non-metropolitan model may be a better option for organizing a city. Or alternatively, an economic decentralized model of metropolitan governance whereby services are placed in corporate structures and the corporations and not necessarily the city reduces the problem of moral hazard.

---

[5] Although a cluster of municipalities facing financial problems may also exhibit the problem of "too big too fail" requiring group bail-out.

Potential bankruptcy and possible bailouts however are better managed through alternative instruments. These include legal, administrative and regulatory systems. New Zealand relies on the legal system. The USA relies on politically established control boards run by the state governments, thus allowing for some separation of powers whereby the state government regulates bankruptcies while the city manages service delivery. South Africa has a municipal regulatory framework that is managed by central government. These different mechanisms allow the structure of urban governance to be determined by efficiency and equity principles leaving macro economic issues to be managed by upper tier governments — similar to the conclusion reached by Musgrave on the policy challenge of stabilizing the macro-economy.

Overall, the different models of governance have different strengths and weaknesses depending on whether the emphasis is on efficiency, equity or macro-economic stability factors. The ultimate choice of the appropriate governance of any city will depend on the weights policy makers place on the different criteria. *For Dhaka we favor the metropolitan approach with appropriate amendments to ensure allocative efficiency. For example, Dhaka can be structured as a two-tiered system of governance or sub-divided into smaller regions or wards under a one-tiered system. A metropolitan system also allows for some form of local redistribution without excessive economic inefficiency. But broader equity and macroeconomic stability considerations are best addressed by central government.*

## 4.4 Managing the Transition: Implementing the Governance Model

Choosing an urban governance structure is a challenging process; implementing the chosen model may be even more daunting. In the case of Johannesburg, the city operated in the context of a *decentralized* unitary government. Johannesburg already had access to finance, functions, and functionaries which the city could manage with limited interference of upper-tiers of government. The challenge was to organize the city but the decision in terms of process and final choice essentially belonged to the policy makers and residents of Johannesburg. The context of Dhaka and Bangladesh is quite different. Bangladesh is a *centralized* unitary country where the central government holds the key decision-making process. Any re-organization of Dhaka will need to combine the challenge of devolution and city-wide restructuring, two processes that would require the direct involvement of central government.

In addition, there are important capacity, political and macro-economic factors that will determine the pace of decentralization. While the challenges facing Dhaka city call for a wholesale change in city governance, political realities and capacity constraints might require an incremental approach to implementation. In this context of incremental change care has to be taken to ensure that each step is a part of the bigger reform vision. What could be elements of a strategic, incremental approach that involves the central government?

- *Sectoral Approach*: This approach focuses on one or two key services. For example, the Central government could start the process of reforming the water board in Dhaka. Several approaches are possible. The city could be divided into three or four areas, each with its own water board. This is a model that has been adopted by Manila and Melbourne for water and by Delhi for electricity. The water boards could then be corporatized and one or two could even involve private sector management. The corporate structures could then be devolved fully to the city or a joint-ownership could be proposed with central government. The principle here is that central government starts the process of service reform in a major sector and then devolves the service to the city rather than devolving the service and leaving the reform process in the hands of the city. This approach can be applied to other areas such as slum upgrading, land management, and transport reform.

  *The sectoral approach ensures that investments continue and technical support for capacity building is possible even during a process of institutional change. What is critical though is that the sectoral approach is not taken in isolation but, instead, is viewed within the context of a dialogue and discussion of the overall governance reform of the city.*

- *Fiscal Approach*: Currently, the fiscal flows to the city from central government entails scheme based funding: conditional grants linked to specific projects. There is limited discretion in the hands of the city level policy makers. As a result capacity and accountability is difficult to foster through these fiscal mechanisms. Central government can begin to consolidate these scheme based fiscal transfers into a combination of unconditional and conditional grants and transferred as block grants to the city. The approach places much more discretion and flexibility in the hands of city managers. To ensure greater accountability, central government can ensure that access to these more flexible funds is linked to improvements in financial management, auditing and procurement.

- *Incentive Approach*: Central government could establish an incentive fund — a challenge fund of sorts, open for all the big city corporations of Bangladesh. The challenge would be for the cities to provide a strategic plan for re-organization of their governance structure and a plan for implementation. Central Government could provide the broad guidelines of the requirement and the incentives involved. This process allows local politics to determine the reform process rather than follow central government dictates. Different cities could then adopt different reform strategies as permitted by their political economy. In addition, the local plans offer a context of catalyzing a dialogue between central and city governments and promote competition between cities. There are different examples of incentive fund mechanism. In South Africa, the "Local Government Restructuring Fund" is managed by the Ministry of Finance and supports governance reforms that are negotiated by local governments and their political leadership in consultation with communities. In India, the National Urban Renewal Mission is more top down and investment oriented in the design of the incentives. While different in their approach, both these funds adopt the common principle that central incentives can play a role in promoting institutional changes at the local level.

- *Consultative Approach*: City reforms are a highly political process — it is not a technocratic exercise. In this context, getting a buy-in from various stakeholders including direct feedback from residents is essential for the credibility and sustainability of the reform process. Engaging in a consultative process, therefore, would be a pre-requisite for initiating a reform process. Most critically, the consultative process would be needed to seek a consensus around the appropriate governance model — the vision — while implementation would evolve around an incremental but strategic path towards achieving this vision.

These various approaches are of course not mutually exclusive. The incentive approach, for example, could make the consultative process mandatory. Conditions of governance changes could be part of the fiscal approach. A sectoral approach could also be linked to the consultative approach. The important point is that these different elements should be seen as a part of implementing a strategic reform of the city governance.

## 4.5 Key Issues Underlying Strategic Choices

The discussion above lays down some basic guiding principles that must underpin a reform of Dhaka city governance. It also provides alternative options and approaches based on a review of good practice international experiences. The different options and approaches discussed above must all be consistent with the fundamental guiding principles and reflect the political realities of what is possible or might work in the political reality of a specific country context.

***Fundamental Principles***: The fundamental reform principles concern the need to —

- establish a decentralized and accountable city government;
- that has well defined service delivery responsibilities;
- has elected government accountable to its residents;
- has considerable financial autonomy; and
- has well defined accountability relationship with the supervising higher level government.

***Design and Implementation Issues***: Consistent with this broad foundation, actual design could vary based on what might work in the specific socio-economic-political environment facing Dhaka city and the capacity to implement reforms. The reform strategy involves a choice of specific service delivery, extent of financial devolution, and the design of the city management in the context of the defined devolution. As we saw above, a range of options including different combinations of specific options is possible. In approaching the reform, the key questions that need to be resolved are as follows.

*Devolution Issues*

- Is the principle that the Mayor and Council should be accountable for the overall management of Dhaka — formulation and implementation of a city strategy — an important guiding premise for the reform of Dhaka?
- If so, what are the key services and tax instruments that should be devolved to the city level from central government in order to ensure that the mayor and the council are accountable to the residents of Dhaka?
- Should user-pays- principle be the key guiding principle for managing the cities finances for all commercial services? Where some departure may be needed on political grounds, how should the subsidy be targeted and what are compensating finance sources?

*City Design Issues*

- What are the alternative models of metropolitan city design that may be applicable for Dhaka?
- How do these rank against the fundamental guiding principles that were established at the outset to assess the reform process?
- What criteria might be used (e.g. a le Musgrave) to choose a particular model for designing Dhaka city management?
- How might one approach city reform to maximize the synergy between public and private sector in delivering city services?

*Implementation Issues*

- What kind of consultation processes can be initiated around the policy of city reforms?
- Should the process of managing a city reform process a top-down (e.g. service approach) or bottom up (e.g. incentive approach) process?
- Is the approach of being strategic but incremental the correct approach for managing city reforms?

# 5. Concluding Remarks

The positive correlation between urbanization and economic growth of a country is one of the constants of development. The relationship between the economic development of Dhaka and that of Bangladesh is not an exception to this rule. As the leading metropolis of the country and one of the world's mega-cities, Dhaka is an economic hub, contributing to over 50 percent of Bangladesh's manufacturing and organized services sector GDP. But increasingly, the problems of service delivery and management suggest that Dhaka city may be contributing below its economic potential. Indeed the service delivery problems of Dhaka suggest that time is running out and an urgent rethinking of the management of the city is essential to avoid a loss of the city's dynamism.

This Monograph suggests that the management problems of Dhaka cannot be addressed in a piece meal fashion. While massive investment will be needed given the large backlog of unmet demand, deployment of additional resources alone will not work. Past experience shows that corruption and mismanagement are serious constraints and unless these are tackled, the effectiveness of additional spending will be limited. As well, given weak fiscal capacity at the national level, much of the new resources will need to come from user fees and greater tax compliance of residents, neither of which will be forthcoming without improved service. So, there is a need to fundamentally and systemically rethink the governance of Dhaka. In this context, the analysis offers some basic guiding principles that must underpin a reform of the city. It provides alternative options and approaches based on a review of good practice international experiences.

The Monograph concludes that in reforming Dhaka policy makers will need to —

- establish a decentralized and accountable city government;
- that has well defined service delivery responsibilities;

- has elected government accountable to its residents;
- has considerable financial autonomy; and
- has well defined relationship with central government.

In sum, Dhaka will need to move towards a well defined city government structure with a strong mayor and council system. Consistent with this broad foundation, actual design will vary based on what might work in the specific social, economic, and political environment of Bangladesh and the Dhaka city. Given the primacy of Dhaka, regardless of the outcome of the forthcoming national elections, the challenge of reforming Dhaka has become a national priority.

The concern that making Dhaka more efficient may be self-defeating if the improved governance of the city leads in turn to "excessive migration" — a vicious cycle of sorts — is not well founded As noted, rural-urban migration is a fact of development. The challenge is not one of stopping the migration process but managing it better. In other words, an efficient Dhaka would be better able to manage the process of in-migration and this may well result in allowing the city to accommodate more migrants. This will happen by improving the functioning of land, housing and transport markets and proper pricing of services and thereby the cost at the margin imposed by new migration could be more effectively passed onto the migrant, thus ensuring a self regulating migration process. Simultaneously, the issue of excessive migration needs to be addressed by understanding the dynamics of the overall urban hierarchy in the country. The support for secondary towns — where the growth is actually increasing — will help balance the allocation of population across the country. This is best undertaken by increasing the productivity of agriculture, which creates the demand for secondary towns through economic linkages. It also occurs by improving the local governance of smaller towns along the same lines as in Dhaka.

# References

Ahmad, Junaid. 1998. "Structure of Urban Governance in South African Cities." *International Tax and Finance.*

Ahmed, Sadiq. 2005. *Transforming Bangladesh into a Middle Income Economy.* New Delhi: Macmillan.

Anam, Shaheen. 1993. *Staying Alive: Urban Poor in Bangladesh.* Dhaka: UNICEF.

Asian Development Bank (ADB). 2004. *Water in Asian Cities — Utilities Performance and Civil Society Views.* Manila: Asian Development Bank.

———. 2001a. *Urban Indicators for Managing Cities: Cities Data Book.* Manila: Asian Development Bank.

———. 2001b. *Urban Transport and Environment Improvement Study.* Final Report. No. ADB TA 3297-BAN. Manila: Asian Development Bank.

———. 2000. *Asian Cities in the 21$^{st}$ Century: Contemporary Approaches to Municipal Management.* Vols. 1-5. Manila: Asian Development Bank.

Asiaweek Online. 2000. *Best Cities in Asia for 2000.* At http://www.asiaweek.com/asiaweek/features/asiacities2000/cities.intro.html.

Bangladesh Bureau of Statistics (BBS). 2004. *Statistical Yearbook of Bangladesh 2002.* Dhaka.

———. 2003. *Statistical Yearbook of Bangladesh 2001.* Dhaka.

———. 2001. *Preliminary Report of the Household Income and Expenditure Survey 2000.* Dhaka.

Buchanan, James. 1975. *The Limits of Liberty: Between Leviathan and Anarchy.* Chicago: University of Chicago Press.

Center for Urban Studies. 2006. *Slums of Urban Bangladesh: Mapping and Census.* Dhaka: National Institute of Population Research and Training.

Chowdhury, Amirul Islam. 2005. *Instruments of Local Financial Reform and Their Impact on Service Delivery — Institutional and Development Concerns: Case Studies of India and Bangladesh.* Available online at http://www.saneinetwork.net/research/sanei_VI/ abstract5.asp.

Dhaka City Corporation (DCC). 2005. Website at http://www.dhakacity.org/.

Government of Bangladesh (GOB). 1998. *The Fifth Five Year Plan 1997-2002*. Dhaka: Ministry of Planning.

International Centre for Municipal Development. 2002. *Urban Sector and Municipal Governance* .Federation of Canadian Municipalities, Ottawa. At http://www.muannepal.org/resourcecenter/FCM/Urban_sector_municipal_governances/Urban_sector_and_municipal_services.pdf.

International Monetary Fund (IMF). 2005. *Government Finance Statistics*. Washington, D.C.

Islam, Nazrul. 2005. *Dhaka Now: Contemporary Urban Development*. Dhaka: Bangladesh Geographical Society.

———. 1996. "City Study of Dhaka." in Jeffrey Stubbs and Giles Clarke (eds.) *Megacity Management in the Asian and Pacific Region*. Vol. 2. Manila: Asian Development Bank.

Karim, Shahriar. 2004. "Clampdown on rickshaws in Dhaka." BBC Online. Website at http://news.bbc.co.uk/2/hi/south_asia/3744218.stm.

Lautier, F. 2006. *Cities in a Globalizing World*, The World Bank Institute, Washington, D.C.

McGee, Terry. 2001. "Urbanization Takes on New Dimensions in Asia's Population Giants." *Population Today*. Vol. 29(7). Washington, D.C.: Population Reference Bureau.

Musgrave, Richard A. 1959. *The Theory of Public Finance*. International Student Edition. Tokyo: McGraw-Hill Kogakusha Ltd.

National Research Council. 2003. *Cities Transformed*. Washington, D.C.: National Academy of Sciences.

Pryer, Jane. 2003. *Poverty and Vulnerability in Dhaka Slums: The Urban Livelihood Study*. England: Ashgate.

Rashid, Salim. 2000. "Compact Townships as a Strategy for Economic Development." *Professional Journal of the Council on Tall Buildings and Urban Habitat*. Vol. 1(3). pp. 8-26.

Romaya, Sam and Carole Rakodi (eds.). 2002. *Building Sustainable Urban Settlements*. London: ITDG Publishing.

Siddiqui, Kamal et.al. 2004. *Mega City Governance in South Asia*. Dhaka: The University Press Limited.

Siddiqui, Kamal. 2000. *Overcoming the Governance Crisis in Dhaka City*. Dhaka: The University Press Limited.

———. 1990. *Social Formation in Dhaka City: A Study in Third World Urban Sociology*. Dhaka: The University Press Limited.

Stubbs, Jeffrey and Clarke, Giles (eds.) *Megacity Management in the Asian and Pacific Region*. Vol. 1 and 2. Manila: Asian Development Bank.

The Economist Intelligence Unit. 2002. "Melbourne and Vancouver are the world's best cities to live in" at http://edition.cnn.com/2002/WORLD/europe/10/04/worldcities.

The Sustainable Development Networking Program (SDNP). 2005. Website: http://www.sdnpbd.org/ sdi/international_days/wed/2005/index.html.

United Nations Center for Human Settlements (Habitat). 2001a. *The State of the World's Cities 2001*. Nairobi: Habitat.

———. 2001b. *Cities in a Globalizing World*. Nairobi: Habitat.

United Nations Human Settlements Program (UN-Habitat). 2004. *The State of the World's Cities 2004/2005*. Nairobi: UN-Habitat.

United Nations. 2003. *World Urbanization Prospects: The 2003 Revision*. Website at http://esa.un.org/unup/.

Water and Sanitation Program. 2001. *Serving Poor Consumers in South Asian Cities*. Overview Paper. No. 23724. New Delhi: Water and Sanitation Program.

———. 1997. *Water vending in Old Dhaka: Balancing Inequities and Making Profits*. Field Note. Dhaka: UNDP/World Bank.

World Bank, Proshika and Survey Research System. 2002. *Bangladesh Urban Service Delivery: A Score Card*. Dhaka.

World Bank. 2006. *Bangladesh: A Strategy for Sustained Growth*. Draft Economic Report. Washington, D.C.: South Asia Poverty Reduction and Economic Management Unit.

———. 2005a. *World Development Indicators 2005*. Washington, D.C.

———. 2005b. *Dhaka Urban Poverty: Land and Housing Issues*. Draft Paper. Washington, D.C.

———. 2005c. *Dhaka and Chittagong Water Supply and Sewerage Project*. Project Information Document. Report No. AB1366. Washington, D.C.

———. 2004a. *Housing Finance Reforms in Bangladesh*. Finance and Private Sector Development. South Asia Region. Washington D.C.

———. 2004b. *Fiscal Decentralization to Rural Governments in India*. New Delhi: Oxford University Press.

———. 2004c. *Power Sector Development Technical Assistance Project*. Project Appraisal Document. Report No. 28848-BD. Washington, D.C.

———. 2003a. *Reaching the Poor through Sustainable Partnerships: The Slum Sanitation Program in Mumbai, India*. Urban Notes. No. 7. Washington, D.C.

———. 2003b. *World Development Report 2004: Making Services Work for Poor People.* Washington, D.C.: Oxford University Press/World Bank.

———. 2002. *Poverty in Bangladesh: Building on Progress.* Report No. 24299-BD. Washington, D.C.

———. 2001. *The Challenge of Urban Government: Policies and Practices.* Washington, D.C.: World Bank Institute.

———. 2000. "Private Provision of a Public Good: Social Capital and Solid Waste Management in Dhaka, Bangladesh." *Policy Research Working Paper* 2422. Washington, D.C.

———. 2000. *Cities in Transition.* Infrastructure and Urban Development Department. Washington, D.C.

———. 1998a. *Dhaka Urban Transport Project (DUTP).* Project Appraisal Document. Report No. 18339-BD. Washington, D.C.

———. 1998b. *Municipal Finance Management Sector Study.* Report No. 16558-BD. Washington, D.C.

# Index

administration
civil, 33; efficiencies of, 45, 47; land, 25
Ahmad, Junaid Kamal, iii, xii, 42, 57
Ahmed, Sadiq, iii, xii, 32, 57
alternative options and approaches, xii, 52, 55
Anam, Shaheen, 57
Asian Development Bank (ADB), 7, 31, 57-9

bailouts, 48, 49
Bangalore, 2, 4, 21
Bangladesh Atomic Energy Commission, 19
Bangladesh Bureau of Statistics (BBS), 1, 10, 12, 27-8, 57
Bangladesh Road Transport Corporation (BRTC), 25-6
Bangladesh Telephone and Telegraph Board (BTTB), 25-6
bankruptcies, 49
basic services, ix, xi, 3, 13, 25, 31; power, 29, 32-4, 37, 41; private providers of, 31, 41
bribery, 16
Buchanan, James, 44, 57
budgets, 27, 31, 43, 47-8
building control, 24

capacity constraints, 50
Capital City Development Agency (RAJUK), 15, 24-7, 39
Center for Urban Studies, 20, 57
Central Government, xii, 24, 30, 39, 41, 47-51, 53, 56

Chief Executive Officer (CEO), 25, 29, 43
Chittagong, 4, 11, 21-2, 48, 59
Chowdhury, Amirul Islam, 57
City Design Issues, 53
City Development Index (CDI), vii, 2
city government, xii, 26, 28, 30, 33, 37, 39, 41-4, 51-2, 55-6; legal framework of, 23, 28; responsibilities of, vii, 30
Clarke, Giles, 58-9
Colombo, 2, 3, 4
control of animals, 24
corruption, xi-xii, 1, 3, 15, 37, 55

decentralization
economic, 43-4; of functions, 38; political, 42-3, 45-6; separation of powers, 49
Delhi, 2-4, 13, 21, 39, 50, 57, 59
Department of Public Health Engineering (DPHE), 26-7
Chief Engineer of, 24
devolution, 30, 37, 41, 50, 52-3
Dhaka City Corporation (DCC), vii, 23-9, 58; poor accountability of, 29; spending by, 27; spending pattern of, 27; staffing of, 27
Dhaka Division, vii, 9-10
per capita expenditure of, 10
Dhaka Electric Supply Company (DESCO), vii, 16, 25
Dhaka Electricity Supply Authority (DESA), vii, 16-7, 24-6
Dhaka Metropolitan Police (DMP), 25
Dhaka Municipal Corporation (DMC), 23; municipal boundaries of, 44; non-metropolitan model of, 48

Dhaka Water and Sewerage Authority (D-WASA), 16-7, 24-7, 32

Dhaka, v-vii, ix, xi-xii, 1-4, 7-29, 32-40, 42, 48-50, 52-3, 55-60; central, 42; core services in, 13; development strategy for, 35; elected and accountable government of, 37; electricity coverage of, 13; empowering municipal governments of, 46; governance of, xii, 55; investment in, xii, 35-7, 51, 55; investment for city services in, 37; labor force in, 13; local government of, 23, 29-30, 33-4, 38, 42, 51; low income city of, xi, 1; making it more livable, 35; mega city, 11, 25, 27; metropolitan governments of, 38, 42-4, 46-8; poverty reduction in, 11; problems of, xii, 55; ranking, 3; reform process for restructuring, 38; reforming, v-vi, xii, 33-5, 50, 52, 55, 56; town planning of, 24; urban planning of, 35; welfare of urban citizens of, 40; well-being of residents of, 39

Dhanmondi, 13, 42

economic linkages, 36, 56

Economist Intelligence Unit (EIU), 2, 59

*Economist*, The, 2

education, 2, 13, 24, 31
  NGOs in the delivery of basic services, 32

electricity, 16, 32
  per capita consumption of, 16

elites, xi, 3

employment, 13, 35

fees
  from advertisements, 26; from cinema, 26; from licenses, 26; licensing of trading, 24

Fifth Five Year Plan, 33, 58

financial autonomy, xii, 23, 29, 34, 37, 52, 56

fiscal mechanisms, 51

fragile environment, xi, 1

functional responsibility, 40

garbage, 20, 32

garments industry, 7, 11

gas services, 32

gender disparity, 32

governance
  appropriate model of, 52; change in city, 50; improvements, 37; urban structure of, 49

Government of Bangladesh (GOB), 33, 48, 58; civil servants of, 24-5, 34; inefficiency and coordination of, 37

Gram Panchayat (GP), 30

grants, iv, 26-8, 34, 50

Gross Domestic Product (GDP), 7, 11-2, 26, 29, 55

groundwater level, 16

Gulshan, 23, 42, 46

health risks, xi, 1

House Building Finance Corporation (HBFC), 15

Household Income and Expenditure Survey, 9, 57

housing, 2, 13-5, 20, 32, 35-6, 56; finance, 13, 15, 32; private, 32; upscale, 15

income opportunities, xi, 1, 11, 35

International Monetary Fund (IMF), 58

Islam, Nazrul, ix, 1, 7, 20, 58

Johannesburg, 39, 43-4, 47-9

Karachi, 2-4, 7

Karim, Shahriar, 58

Karnataka, 31

Kerala, 30

Khulna, 11, 21-2

Kolkata, 1, 13, 21, 31

Lagos, 3, 7

Lahore, 2

land
  fills, 44; grabbing, 15; limited, xi, 1; residential values of, 13
Lautier, F., 23, 58
Local Government Law, 23

management
  centralized, 29; land, 39-40, 50; mismanagement, xii, 55; rethinking of, 55; structure of, 23-4, 26, 29; traffic, xi, 1, 3, 19, 32, 38, 40
Manila Water Board, 39
Manila, 4, 39, 50, 57-9
Mayor, 23-4, 29, 53
McGee, Terry, 58
Melbourne, 47, 50, 59
metropolitan
  approach, 49; model, 42-3, 47; organization, 46; system, 46-7, 49
migration, xi, 1, 7, 12, 36, 56; in-migration, 36, 56; process, 36, 56; rural-urban, 36, 56
Ministry of Power, 25
Minneapolis-St. Paul, 44, 46-7
Mirpur, 23
money
  extortions and protection of, 21; illegal, 15
Motijheel, iv, 46
motorized vehicle, 19
Mumbai, 2-4, 21, 31, 59
municipalities, 23, 32-3, 42-4, 46-8, 58
Musgrave, Richard A., 45, 48-9, 53, 58

National Research Council, 58
Nationalized Commercial Banks (NCBs), 15
Nigeria, 7
Non-Motorized Transport (NMT), vii, 19
non-poor household, 22

piped water, 16, 32
planning criterion, 45
planning efficiency, 45

policy intervention, 48
political instability, xi, 4
political realities, 50, 52
pollution
  air, xi, 1, 17, 19; lead, 19
pooling fiscal resources, 47
population, xi, 1, 7-9, 13, 16-7, 20, 35-6, 56
Pourashaba Ordinance, 24
poverty
  line, 9, 20; national urban rate, 10
Power Development Board (PDB), 16
projects
  fly-over, 40; implementation of, 33
property
  rights, 15, 39; sale of, 26
Pryer, Jane, 20, 58
Public Affairs Center (PAC), 21
public
  finance, 38, 39, 43, 45; health, 20, 24; works, 25

Rajshahi, 21-2
Rakodi, Carole, 58
Rashid, Salim, 58
recreational activities, 2
reform(s)
  basic guiding principles of, xii, 52, 55; capacity to implement, 52; challenge of, xii, 4; city reform strategy, 37; fundamental principles of, 52; implementation issues of, 52-3; key constraints of, 5, 37; lack of commitment to, 33; principles of, vi, 36
rents from markets, 26
resource base, 26, 29
results of survey, 22
revenue collection, 30
rickshaws, 18-9, 58
Romaya, Sam, 58

sanitation, 17-8, 21-2, 31, 37-8
service delivery, xii, 1, 22, 27, 32, 38, 40, 42-3, 46, 49, 52, 55

Siddiqui, Kamal, ix, 2, 23-4, 29, 58
slum(s), xi, 1, 3, 15, 20-1, 31, 35, 50; dwellers, xi, 3, 20-1, 31; living conditions of, 21; settlements, 20
solid waste, 18, 38, 43-4
South Asian mega cities, 1, 7
Stubbs, Jeffrey, 58-9
Suspended Particulate Matter (SPM), 19
Sustainable Development Networking Program (SDNP), 59

taxes
  local, 43; personal property, 44; property, 26, 41, 44
Titas Gas, 25
toilet blocks, 31
Toronto, 42
traffic
  congestion, 19, 35, 40; nightmare, 19; problem, 35; urban, xi, 1
transport, 12, 19, 21-2, 26, 32, 36-8, 40, 46, 50, 56-7, 60
travel mode, 18

UN-Habitat, 4, 59
UNICEF, 57
Union Parishads, 34
United Nations Development Program (UNDP), 33, 59
urbanization, xi, 1, 5, 13, 35-6, 55; reflection of, 35
Uttara, 42

ward commissioner, 23-4, 29
ward members, 29
Washington DC, iv, 42
water supply, 22, 24, 31-2, 37; reliability of, 35
*Weekly Asiaweek*, The, 3
World Bank, iv, ix, 7, 10-16, 20-22, 31, 33, 35, 41, 58-60
World Bank, Proshika and Survey Research System, 59
World Bank-Proshika survey, 16